POEMS OF GUIDO GEZELLE

POEMS OF GUIDO GEZELLE

A BILINGUAL ANTHOLOGY

EDITED BY PAUL VINCENT

UCLPRESS

This edition published in 2016 by
UCL Press
University College London
Gower Street
London WC1E 6BT

First published in 1999 by the UCL Centre for Low Countries Studies

Available to download free: www.ucl.ac.uk/ucl-press

Text © Paul Vincent, 2016

A CIP catalogue record for this book is available
from The British Library.

This book is published under a Creative Commons
Attribution Non-commercial 4.0 International license
(CC BY-NC 4.0). This licence allows you to share and
adapt the work for non-commercial use providing author
and publisher attribution is clearly stated, and any changes
are indicated. Further details about CC BY licenses are
available at http://creativecommons.org/ licenses/

ISBN: 978-1-910634-92-9 (Hbk.)
ISBN: 978-1-910634-93-6 (Pbk.)
ISBN: 978-1-910634-94-3 (PDF)
ISBN: 978-1-910634-95-0 (epub)
ISBN: 978-1-910634-96-7 (mobi)
ISBN: 978-1-911307-85-3 (html)
DOI: 10.14324/111.9781910634943

FOREWORD

WHY COMMEMORATE GEZELLE?

PAUL VINCENT

GUIDO GEZELLE

> Plant
> fountain
> shoot that roots
> jet that spatters
> tempest above all deeps
> storm across all plains
> wild rosetrees blow
> stems of alder catkins bare
>
> Deepest distance
> farthest depth
>
> calyx that quivers in the cup of both my palms
> and darling as the daisy
> As the poppy red
> O my wild poppy
>
> Paul van Ostaijen (1896–1928), translated by James Holmes

This acclamation of Gezelle by an Expressionist of a succeeding generation is typical of the awe with which he has been regarded in his home culture. The writer August Vermeylen sees his significance for Flemish literature in biblical terms – that the poet himself would have no doubt found blasphemous: 'In the beginning was Gezelle; and Gezelle was the Word ...'[1]

However, amid the polemics and recriminations that seem inescapable accompaniments to literary commemorations nowadays, the Flanders-based Dutch writer Benno Barnard recently sparked controversy by suggesting that Gezelle had little to say to him as a reader at the end of the twentieth century.[2] Invidious comparisons were made between the official funds being lavished on the Gezelle centenary and the less generous subsidy afforded the twentieth anniversary of the death of the 'worthier' irreverent modernist Louis-Paul Boon (1912–79).[3] The puzzled outside observer might wonder why it has to be Gezelle *or* Boon, and why this tiny corner of Europe that produced two extraordinary originals cannot rejoice in its own cultural richness and diversity.

There are more encouraging signs: it is refreshing to see that the commemorative exhibition organised by the poet's home town of Bruges celebrates not only the pious regionalist and nationalist icon, but also the polyglot cosmopolitan, as reflected in his extensive library.[4]

The English reader without Dutch has no need to grope for a context for much of Gezelle's work: his love of regional speech and folklore, and his attraction for the minute details of nature that he shares with Robert Burns (1759–96), like Gezelle a gardener's son. His Franciscan sense of the brotherhood of Nature sometimes suggests the poetry of John Clare (1793–1860), while the devotional dimension and formal experiment (for example, onomatopoeia) suggest the sprung rhythms and spiritual questing of fellow priest Gerard Manley Hopkins (1844–89). The Anglophile Gezelle visited England several times on church duties, and one can only speculate on the impact Hopkins's work might have had on Gezelle, had it been published during his lifetime. Kindred spirits, and in the case of Burns a possible partial influence – but Gezelle, great writer that he was, is much more than the sum of influences. It is hard to dissent from Jozef Deleu's comments in a recent anthology:

> There is no poet who has made our language sing in such an incomparable way. The wonder of the poet Gezelle is his gift of wonderment. Childlike and naive, he spends his life in the midst of nature. He has no explanation for all the wonders that strike his eye and ear, but throughout his life they move him to praise the Creator. Gezelle is always uninhibited and unrestrained in his rapture. When he is overwhelmed by solitude and sadness, his language is just as musical as when he is in joyful mood. His poetry is carried by

a Romantic sense of life, but lucidity and simplicity are its most essential features. Gezelle the poet is both a seeker and a finder. Whatever he touches with his word, regains the purity of the first day. That makes him unique.[5]

In selecting poems for the present anthology, my aim was to give as representative a picture as possible of Gezelle's large poetic output (based on source-language anthologies, critical views and personal preferences), from devotional, through narrative to celebratory and expressionistic. I also wished to include as wide as possible a spectrum of translators in English. It is particularly gratifying to be able to include a number of expert dialect versions, two in Lowland Scots ('Twa Aivers' and 'To...?') and one Yorkshire-flavoured ('Farmer Nick'). What this volume cannot, of course, do is do justice to the range and versatility of 'the at least five Gezelles' identified by André Lefevere (journalist, linguist, educator, priest, experimental poet).[6] I can only offer a window on the last and, arguably, greatest of these: the lyric poet.

The bibliographies appended are intended to assist those wishing to explore the poetry and its translation into English in greater depth. We trust that the poems will retain at least some of their capacity to charm, arrest and move in English versions.

NOTES
1. A. Vermeylen, *De Vlaamse letteren van Gezelle tot heden*, Hasselt, 1963, p. 5.
2. *Knack*, 27 January 1999.
3. Cf. Tom Naegels, *De Morgen*, 28 December 1998. For some more measured reactions, see the Gezelle feature in *Standaard der Letteren*, 6 May 1999.
4. 'Reizen in den geest'. De boekenwereld van Guido Gezelle. Biekorfbibliotheek, Bruges, 30 April–10 July 1999; University College London, 22–7 November 1999.
5. Jozef Deleu (ed.), *Waar zit die heldere zanger? De mooiste gedichten van Guido Gezelle*, Tielt: Lannoo, 1998.
6. In L. Henderson (ed.), *Reference Guide to World Literature*, 2 vols. New York/London: St. James Press, 1995, I, p. 465.

ACKNOWLEDGEMENTS

Unless otherwise stated, all textual references are to J. Boets (ed.), *Guido Gezelle, Volledig Dichtwerk* (Jubileumuitgave). Tielt: Pelckmans & Lannoo, 1998.

I should like to thank the editors of *The Low Countries* for permission to reprint, in slightly amended form, Piet Couttenier's article, originally entitled 'O this is a place!', which first appeared in that journal (1993–4, 137–43), and the editors of *Dutch Crossing: Journal of Low Countries Studies* for permission to use the late André Lefevere's 'Translating a National Monument' (*DC* 12, August 1980, 27–33). Paul Claes and Christine D'haen generously gave their permission for a number of their joint translations to be used.

I am most grateful to Frits Niessen for his helpful advice on the bibliography and for permission to use material he had gathered as part of his ongoing project on translations of Dutch poetry into English, French and German, as well as to Marcus de Schepper of the Royal Library, Brussels, and to Dr A.J.M. Broos of the University of Ann Arbor, Michigan, for supplying invaluable information and a number of texts unavailable in the UK.

Thanks are due to the Ministry of the Flemish Community, Culture Administration, Brussels, for its generous support for this publication, and to the Centre for Dutch and Flemish Culture, University College London, for arranging the launch of the book and an associated one-day translation workshop at UCL in November 1999.

(PV)

ON THE NEW EDITION

The only change I wish to make to the original selection of translations is to substitute two remarkable dialect versions of the classic poems 'Het schrijverke' (p. 64) and 't Er viel 'ne keer' (p. 90). These are by Edwin Morgan (Glaswegian) and Francis Jones (North Yorkshire) respectively and first appeared in *Dutch Crossing: Journal of Low Countries Studies*, 24/1, Summer 2000, pp. 39–54. They bring a special resonance to the originals. Thanks to Francis Jones and to the Edwin Morgan Estate for permission to republish the two translations here.

PAUL VINCENT

CONTENTS

PIET COUTTENIER   Introduction
                             The English World of Guido Gezelle   1

ANDRÉ LEFEVERE   Translating a National Monument   8

Chronology of Gezelle's Life and Work   14

TEN VERSIONS OF 'O LIED'   15

POEMS AND TRANSLATIONS
Poems in chronological order (*previously unpublished translation)   **39**

1848
De Mandelbeke   40
The Mandel Stream (fragment, Swepstone)   41

1852
Aanroepinge   42
Reply in Verses (Van Eyken)*   43

1855
Boodschap van de vogels en andere opgezette dieren   44
Message from the Birds and Other Stuffed Animals (Van Eyken)*   45
De averulle en de blomme   60
The Cockchafer and the Flower (Vincent)*   61
Timpe, tompe, terelink   62
Hyder Iddle Diddle Dum (Lovelock)*   63

1857
Het schrijverke (Gyrinus natans)   64
The Watter-Scriever (Gyrinus natans) (Morgan)   65
O 't ruischen van het ranke riet   68

Oh! The Rustling of the Slender Reed (Swepstone)	69
Aan de leeuwerke in de lucht	70
To the Lark in the Sky (Vincent)*	71

1858

Ik droome alreê	76
I Dream E'en Now (Vincent)*	77
Een bonke keerzen kind	78
A Bunch of Cherries, Child (Holmes)	79
Dien avond en die rooze	82
That Evening and That Rose (Stillman)	83
In de blanke lonken	84
In the White Moon Winking (Claes/D'haen)	85
Zilverblanke zwanen	86
Silvery White Swans (Vincent)*	87
Rammentati	88
Rammentati (Van Eyken)*	89

1859

't Er viel 'ne keer …	90
A Little Leaf Once Fluttered … (Jones)	91
Wie zijt gij	94
What Are You? (Van Eyken)*	95
Ik misse u	96
I Miss You (Vincent)*	97
Een dreupel poesij	98
A Drop of Poetry (King)*	99
God is daar	100
God is There (Van Eyken)*	101
Als de ziele luistert	102
When the Soul Listens (Swepstone)	103
Ter inleidinge	102
Introduction (Vincent)*	103
Kerkhofblommen	106
Churchyard Flowers (fragment, Van Eyken)*	107
Gij badt op eenen berg	106
You Prayed on the Mountainside, Alone (Brockway)	107

PAUL VINCENT xi

Blijdschap	108
Joy (Roosbroeck)	109
Hoort 't is de wind	110
Hark! It's the Wind (Van Eyken)	111
'k Hoore tuitend' hoornen	110
Hark, Bugles Are Calling (Lovelock)*	111
Boerke Naas	112
Farmer Nick (Jones)*	113
Slaapt, slaapt, kindtje slaapt	116
Sleep, Baby, Sleep! (Van Eyken)*	117

1860
Gelukkig kind	118
Happy Child (King)*	119
's Avonds	120
Evening (Van Eyken)*	121
Daar liep een dichtje in mijn gebed	120
A Little Verse Ran through My Prayer (King)*	121
Gij zegt dat 't Vlaamsch te niet zal gaan	120
You Say That Flemish Soon Will Die (Irons)	121
Tot de zonne	122
To the Sun (Bithell)	123
Hoe stille is 't als de donder dreegt	124
How Still before the Thunder Comes (Van Eyken)	125
Niet	124
Nothing (Van Eyken)*	125

1861
't zij vroeg of laat	126
Right Soon or Late (Van Eyken)	127

1862
't Laatste	126
The Last (Vincent)*	127
Hangt nen truisch	130
Hang a Sash (Vincent)*	131

1866
Heidensch lied 130
Pagan Song (Van Eyken) 131

1870
Halleluja 132
Hallelujah (Van Eyken)* 133

1872
Verloren moeite 134
Wasted Effort (Van Eyken) 135

1877
O dichtergeest 134
O Poetry (Vincent)* 135
En durft gij mij 136
And Do You Dare (Vincent)* 137

1879
De Vlaamsche taal 138
Our Flemish Speech (Barnouw) 139

1880
O vrienden 138
O Friends (Van Eyken) 139

1882
O wilde en overvalschte pracht 140
O Wild and Perfect Harmony (Van Eyken)* 141
Wat hangt gij daar te praten 144
What Is It Then Attracts Thee (Swepstone) 145

1883
Mijn hert is als een blomgewas 144
My Heart Is Like a Tender Flower (Swepstone) 145

PAUL VINCENT xiii

1886
Drie dingen | 146
Three Burdens (Van Eyken)* | 147

1888
De nachtegalen klinken | 148
The Nightingales Are Calling (Hare) | 149

1890
O blomme | 150
O Flower (Van Eyken)* | 151

1891
Moederken | 150
Little Mother (Swepstone)* | 151
Zonnewende | 152
Sunspurge (Lovelock)* | 153

1892
Verloren is 't gepijnd | 154
We Strive in Vain (Van Eyken)* | 155

1893
Fiat Lux | 156
Fiat Lux (Van Eyken)* | 157
't Avondt, 't Avondt; traag en treurig | 158
Evening Slowly Veils the Skies (Van Eyken) | 159
Naar het kribbeken des heeren | 160
The Crib (Van Eyken)* | 161
De ramen | 162
Church Window (Van Eyken) | 163
O leeksken licht | 164
O Leak of Light (Claes/D'haen) | 165
'k En ete niet, of 't gene ik ete | 166
I Never Eat but What I Eat (Claes/D'haen) | 167

1894
Den ouden brevier   168
The Old Breviary (Vincent)*   169
Hoe zeere vallen ze af   170
How Soon They All Drop Down (Vincent)*   171

1895
Slapende botten   174
Sleeping Buds (Claes/D'haen)   175

1896
Casselkoeien   176
The Cassel Cows (Swepstone)   177
Hier ben ik   178
Here Am I (Van Eyken)*   179
Wintermuggen   180
Winter Midges (Claes/D'haen)   181
Tranen   182
Tears (Claes/D'haen)   183

1897
Jam Sol Recedit   184
Iam sol recedit (Claes/D'haen)   185
Twee horsen   186
Twa Aivers (Lovelock)*   187
Bonte abeelen   188
The Aspen Tree (Bithell)   189
Winterstilte   188
Winter Quiet (Bithell)   189
Gierzwaluwen (Cypselus Apus)   190
Swifts (Cypselus Apus)   191
Op krukken   192
Yearning (Van Eyken)   193
Juvabit!   200
Comfort (Van Eyken)*   201
Jordane van mijn hert   200
Oh, Jordan of My Heart (Vincent)*   201

PAUL VINCENT   xv

Klopt het om de messe	208
The Church Calls Us All to Mass (Van Eyken)*	209
In Speculo	210
In Speculo (Claes/D'haen)	211

1898

Ego Flos ...	212
Ego Flos ... (Weevers)	213
'k En hoore u nog niet	216
I Cannot Hear You Yet (Vincent)*	217
Slaaplied	218
Christmas Lullaby (Van Eyken)*	219
Voorbij ...	220
To...? (Lovelock)*	221
Aan ...?	222
To ...?	223

Poems originally in English

To a Friend on the Eve of May 1858	224
Arise Ye Flemings! (fragment)	225
Full Fifty Years	225
O Holy Pathmos	225
Ladies and Gentlemen	226
May Your Friends	227
Key to Translators	228
Bibliography of English Translations of Gezelle	229
Lists of Published Translations	233
Bibliography of Secondary Literature on Gezelle in English	234

INTRODUCTION

THE ENGLISH WORLD OF GUIDO GEZELLE

PIET COUTTENIER

Guido Gezelle, born in Bruges in 1830, left a varied œuvre as a man of letters, journalist, translator and populariser. But it is mainly as a poet that he occupies an illustrious position in the history of Dutch literature. He is undoubtedly the most innovative and original Flemish poet between 1680 and 1880. With his exceptional lyrical poetry he was some twenty years ahead of the renewal movement of the so-called Men of the Eighties at the end of the nineteenth century.

His professional career as a priest was a fairly modest one; he became a teacher, a parish priest and the director of a convent. Nevertheless he exerted a considerable influence on younger generations of writers and intellectuals, first as the inspiration behind a national cultural movement in Flanders which linked Flemish identity to folk traditions, language and the Christian religion. Only after his death in 1899 was he fully appreciated as a poet, by both traditionalists and modernists. In Flanders particularly myths also grew up around him.

Compared with the poetry of his contemporaries, his Romantic and religious nature lyrics have a strikingly personal and natural character. His apparently simple poems conceal a sophisticated prosody and a dialogue with spiritual and literary tradition. Their language is complex and diverges from the standardised usage of his environment. Gezelle enriched his idiom with an intensive and life-long study of the Old Dutch (Flemish) language, whose creative potential he activates in his poetry. His favourite themes are childhood, the Flemish landscape, friendship, nature religion, the Flemish vernacular and poetry. He explores nature down to its minutest details and discovers an infinite dimension within it based on his own world of experience. At the same time nature symbolises his own psyche. In addition he wrote a great deal of occasional poetry.

His work has also repeatedly been linked with both British and American literature and culture. And not without reason. After all, Gezelle

PAUL VINCENT   1

was not merely a writer in the native tradition of religious literature dating back to the seventeenth-century Reformation; he was also associated with an international cultural movement of Catholic revival of his day. With regard to England this means that his poetry and prose show affinities with the so-called Oxford Movement, which in a spiritual sense provided a significant response to the scepticism of the Victorian age. The publication of Gezelle's remarkable translation of the then hugely popular *Hiawatha* by Henry Wadsworth Longfellow merely reinforces this 'English connection'. Speculation concerning this has continually been supported by Gezelle's biography, which shows that the poet and priest had contact with England for virtually his entire career.

FLEMISH ANGLOPHILIA

The young Gezelle, educated for the priesthood in the predominantly Catholic West Flanders of the nineteenth century, was exposed very early to the Continental idea, then current, that England was a country to which missionaries should be sent. For that matter many of the buildings in the medieval city of his birth, Bruges, bore witness to the history of English Catholicism. It is symbolic that he should end his career as the chaplain of the renowned English convent there, founded in 1629 by a community of Canon nuns belonging to the Windesheim congregation which had fled from England to settle ultimately in Leuven. Ever since the sixteenth century Bruges, along with such towns as Douai and St Omer in northern France, had been one of the centres of those English concentrations that had sprung up on the Continent in response to the banning of Catholicism in Anglican England. After the French Revolution refugees began a movement in the opposite direction, attempting in turn to convert the Anglican world. The young and extremely idealistic priest Gezelle wanted nothing more than to join in this tradition and this adventure.

Bruges had an extensive so-called English colony: Anglicans – to the Catholic authorities a veritable missionary zone in their own midst – but later also a great many resettled Catholics, some of whom, from the 1850s onwards, would also introduce the artistic ideas of the neo-Gothic revival. It was at the preparatory seminary at Roeselare that the student Gezelle was really introduced to Anglophilia – the educational institute had a separate department or course (*cours*) for English students. Letters have shown that the linguistically talented Gezelle was much sought after by the English lads (*assiégé par les Anglais*), and through the exotic tales and testimonies of heroic pioneers there gradually developed a virtual propaganda campaign on behalf of the missions in England and North America. When Gezelle returned to Roeselare in 1854 as a teacher, it was obvious he would be put in charge of the English students. And there he became friends with Joseph Algar, Master of Arts at Oxford, who on an intellectual level opened many doors for Gezelle. Until 1860, Gezelle engaged in relentless activities on behalf of England. In a relationship characterised by great openness, friendship and trust, he counselled the rather turbulent group of English students, including the non-Catholics, both materially and spiritually. With some of them an extensive exchange developed; concerned mothers in England entered into correspondence with the 'guardian of their boys'. Reinforced by the news of a shortage of priests in England, and supported by the enthusiastic letters of former students who were participating there in the 'great work in the Lord's vineyard', Gezelle developed an unrelenting campaign among his pupils to recruit missionaries. It was a world of idealism, emotion and wishful thinking, as well as one fraught with difficulties with parents and government authorities. Gezelle received many letters from young 'missionaries', expressing both their hope and their confusion after their confrontation with a totally unfamiliar, hostile world.

The odd thing about Gezelle's position was his inability to realise his own dream. His definitive departure for England remained an unfulfilled expectation, interiorised in a number of texts (letters and poetry). He and those around him were for a long time convinced that he would receive permission to go. Repeatedly denied requests made to the Bruges episcopate by Gezelle and others do not seem to have dampened his enthusiasm. In 1861, he wrote to the Dutch man of letters J.A. Alberdingk Thijm that the latter could not imagine how Flemish youth was burning to realise the papal ideal of conversion 'as far as the four corners of the globe'. It was in this atmosphere that Gezelle had been working since 1856, translating Longfellow's 'Mondamin', the fifth canto from *Hiawatha* and the famous poem 'Excelsior', texts informed by a highly ultramontane, anti-Protestant spirit. If it had to be done in this manner, then Gezelle wished to take part in the heroic reconquest of England (and thus the world) as a poet, an act which he and many others felt was an appropriate reciprocal gesture to those who had spread Catholicism on the Continent.

Gezelle's 'English' career continued beyond 1860. Inspired by the English school system, which, among other things, allowed students more freedom, and together with his friend Algar, he co-directed a kind of English department of the Bruges college. In 1861 he became vice rector of the English Seminary, originally a private initiative by a wealthy Catholic convert, John Sutton, but which since its founding in 1859 had been as much a product of cooperation between Bruges and Westminster. Gezelle then came into contact with the English clerical hierarchy, even with Cardinal Wiseman, and now directly prepared the English recruits, who were willing, as we read somewhere, 'to spend time, labour, anxiety and care on their duty'. Gezelle, by then a parish priest in Bruges, remained also after 1865 closely linked with England. He was not only a spiritual guide in the private lives of English families, but also a kindred spirit in a circle of resident foreign artists and archaeologists (James Weale, Thomas Harper King, William Brangwyn, etc.) who, inspired by the ideas of Augustus Welby Pugin, would greatly influence Flemish neo-Gothicism as practised by Jean Baptiste Béthune, Louis Grossé, Jacques Petyt and others.

SACRED POETRY
In a letter dated October 1861, Algar warned his friend Gezelle: 'Don't let your Anglomania be carried too far.' It is a small indication of the fact that Gezelle, confronted with the sober and rationally inclined Algar, still adhered to a strongly romantic, idealistic realm that was no doubt far removed from Victorian England. Someone like Gezelle, from his vantage point in Flanders in the 1850s and 1860s, mainly had an eye for the euphoria that accompanied Catholic emancipation. That specific situation (the small missionary community, often made up of immigrants) demanded the establishment and expansion of a local rural church with a large contribution by educated lay people. This was diametrically opposed to the establishment of a central governing hierarchy (1850) and the worldwide evolution of an ultramontane Catholicism. In fact, Catholic England in the 1850s was riven with controversy. An important role in this was played by the so-called Oxford Movement, originally a kind of counter reformation within Anglicanism, intended to rid it of excess Protestantism. From 1845 onwards it formed the axis of the English variant of a liberal Catholicism striving to raise the intellectual level and freedom of thought of English Catholics, with John Henry Newman as its leading exponent.

It is not always clear to what extent the West Flemish priest Gezelle was aware of these situations, and how far he was capable of expressing any sympathy he may have had for a more liberal form of Catholicism. We know from witnesses that Gezelle both knew and read Cardinal Newman (whom Gezelle's former student Hendrik van Doorne says Gezelle considered 'The New Man'). From fragments and a manuscript of an unfinished poem we know that in 1879, when Newman's honour had been restored by the hierarchy, Gezelle began translating the *Dream of Gerontius* (1860), well known in English Catholic circles. Anyone who reads Gezelle's work, however, will encounter mainly those figures from the same English circles who adhered more strongly to the authority of superiors within the Roman Catholic Church. Furthermore, in its mental outlook Gezelle's work strongly resembles that of the members of the Oxford Movement in their resistance to a secularised world and their rediscovery of the lost institutional power, spirituality and piety of the 'Gothic' Middle Ages. It is also remarkable that, just like Gezelle, John Keble and Frederick William Faber made the link with poetry. In contrast to a poet like Gerard Manley Hopkins, who regarded this relation as problematic, for these poets religion and poetry were extensions of one another. In both areas of experience there is room for the discovery of the sacred via the profane, for the interest in devotion, liturgy, ceremony and tradition.

It is understandable, therefore, that Gezelle too was interested in the 'sacred poetry' of Keble and Faber. It is no coincidence that Gezelle's own first volume of poetry, *Flemish Poetical Exercises* of 1858, contained a translation from Faber's *Hymns* (1849). Also, it is sufficiently well known that the atmosphere around the 'confraternity', a secret society set up by Gezelle for his pupils at the Roeselare minor seminary to promote sacramental devotion, showed striking affinities with the ideas espoused in Faber's *All for Jesus* (1853), a work which circulated among Gezelle's students. In this connection, it is not surprising that Gezelle was euphoric when writing to his favourite student, Eugeen van Oye, from Arundel, where he had been staying as chaplain to the Duchess of Norfolk, recalling the place where Faber situated his *Ethel's Book; or, Tales of the Angels* (1858): 'I am in the very place where "Ethel" lives, at the residence of the Duchess of Norfolk, the mother of the child for whom Ethel's book was written. I have dined with Ethel, spoken to her, heard her speak. I know the houses where the real children lived that are described by Faber; I know the history of Ethel's book. Oh, this is a place! a Catholic duchess in England is something indeed!'

LONGFELLOW

The similarities mentioned above do not alter the fact that there are also great differences between Gezelle's own poetic practice and that of Keble, for that matter probably England's bestselling poet of the nineteenth century. Gezelle's own poetry undergoes a perilous adventure with language, while Keble's, which incidentally is more poetic treatise than actual poems, is more of a blend of theology, devotion and apology in which spontaneity is subdued.

With a poet like Gezelle the situation is somewhat different. This is obvious when we examine Gezelle's most important translation work from 1886 – we shall not consider his prose translations of such Oxford Movement authors as John Mason Neale and Charlotte Yonge – his poetic version of *The Song of Hiawatha*, an epic poem by the popular American poet Henry Wadsworth Longfellow. The exotic tale of a mythical hero, a kind of Messiah bestowing peace and prosperity upon his people, based on hybrid elements from Indian oral culture, was enormously popular in nineteenth-century Europe. Only a year after its American publication, in 1856, Gezelle was one of the first to translate the fifth canto, 'Hiawatha's Fasting', which because of its theme and symbolism (the creation of maize) must certainly have appealed to the young, religiously inspired poet. It is notable that the epic continued to fascinate Gezelle.

Gradually, however, the emphasis shifted from the functionality of the theme to the work of translation itself. He prompted student poets from his surroundings – such as Hugo Verriest and Emiel Lauwers – to try their hand at translation and was in turn stimulated by their results into improving his own 'rendition'. The results of 1886 approached the ideal Gezelle himself had posited in a letter to a colleague (his name was Eugeen de Lepeleer) who in 1889 had just embarked, following in Gezelle's footsteps, on a translation of Friedrich Wilhelm Weber's *Thirteen Lindens* (Dreizehnlinden, 1878). 'You've stuck too close to the German text,' wrote Gezelle; 'you must forget about it, and once it's forgotten, you must polish your own work and file it down *ad amussim.*' For his own literary, aestheticizing translation Gezelle sought his own idiom and rhythm, which indeed often make one forget the original. At the end of the day, for Gezelle, as for many other great and professionally competent poets all too aware of the existence of other texts, translation was ultimately a matter of one's own artistic achievement.

Translated by Scott Rollins

BIBLIOGRAPHY

Baur, Frank, 'Bio-bibliografische inleiding' (Bio-bibliographical Introduction), in: *Guido Gezelle. The Song of Hiawatha. Jubileumuitgave van Guido Gezelles volledige werken* (Guido Gezelle. The Song of Hiawatha. Jubilee Edition of Guido Gezelle's Complete Works), Brussels-Amsterdam: N.V. Standaard Boekhandel, 18 vols, 1930–9, pp. 235–69.

Biervliet, L. van, 'Dear Old Bruges: The English Colony in Bruges in the Nineteenth Century', *The Low Countries* 1998–99, 52–9.

Couttenier, Piet, 'Gezelles onvoltooide vertaling van Newmans *Dream of Gerontius*' ('Gezelle's Uncompleted Translation of Newman's *Dream of Gerontius*'), *Gezelliana*, xiii, i 984, Couttenier (ed.) Anthology, Antwerp: Poeziecentrum, 1997, pp. 106–16,

D'haen, Christine, *De wonde in 't hart. Guido Gezelle: een dichtersbiografie* (The Wound in the Heart. Guido Gezelle: A Poet's Biography), Tielt: Lannoo, 1987.

Gezelle, Guido, *Mijn dichten, mijn geliefde* (My Poems, My Beloved) (Anthology, ed. Piet Couttenier), Ghent, 5th ed., 1997.

Holmes, J. D., *More Roman than Rome: English Catholicism in the Nineteenth Century*, London/ Shepherdtown: Burns and Oates, 1978.

Leeuw, Boudewijn de, et al., *De briefwisseling van Guido Gezelle met de Engelsen 1854–1899* (Guido Gezelle's Correspondence with the English 1854–99), Ghent: Koninklijke Academie voor Nederlandsche taal- en letterkunde 1991.

Nuis, Hermine van, *Guido Gezelle. Flemish Poet-Priest*, New York: Greenwood, 1986.

Persyn, Jan, '*The Song of Hiawaiha* in het spoor van Longfellow' ('The *Song of Hiawatha* in Longfellow's Footsteps'), in: Gezelle, Guido, *The Song of Hiawatha. Tijdkrans. Verzameld dichtwerk 3* (The Song of Hiawatha. A Garland for the Year. Collected Poetry 3), Antwerp / Amsterdam:De Nederlandsche Boekhandel 1981, pp. 9–40.

Richards, Bernhard, *English Poetry of the Victorian Period 1830–1890*, London /New York: Longman, 1988.

Westerlinck, Albert, *Taalkunst van Guido Gezelle* (Guido Gezelle's Verbal Art), Bruges/ Nijmegen: Orion, 1980.

TRANSLATING A NATIONAL MONUMENT

ANDRÉ LEFEVERE

I think that of all the activities open to those who like to think of themselves as literary scholars, translation is the most scientific. I know this goes against all received opinion, and yet if one accepts, with current philosophy of science, that the demarcation line between the scientific and the non-scientific is inter-subjective testability, it is easy to see that what a translator does to a literary text is much more easily testable than what a critic, for example, does to it. I try to translate accordingly. I believe that what I should do is to give readers the most complete set of materials for their concretization of the text. How they use them (i. e. what the text eventually comes to signify for them) is none of my business. I have no poetics of my own to justify distortions of the source text; what is more, I am not allowed to have one. Again contrary to received opinion, I do not create: I transmit. What I do is as 'artistic' or 'non-artistic' as what any translator of any text does. Of course I have to know about literature in order to translate it, but does that give me the right to call myself a 'literary' translator and cordon myself off from the common herd? Others have to know about chemistry, say, or biology in order to be able to translate a text. Does that make them 'chemical' or 'biological' translators? The main thing to me is what is now more and more called the 'pragmatics' of the text, which roughly amounts to what used to be called something like its 'total impact'. This means that I try to find out what effect a text makes on its readers in the original language. But that is not the end of it. I also try to imagine, in some cases, what effect it could have, and I try to find ways to remedy the fact that it does not have that effect. This also means that I translate texts, not words or sentences. It means, moreover, that I translate texts written by very specific writers at a very specific time, not 'anonymous' texts.

If I am lucky, I may be able to influence, to a certain extent, what is grandiloquently called 'the constitution of the canon of world literature', which, in practice, means literature available in English (and/or in Russian).

There may be very specific writers who I may consider to have been – not unjustly, for the term 'justice' carries no weight in these matters – omitted from the canon of world literature. If they are my contemporaries I can probably achieve something because that part of the system is still evolving, still constituting itself. If they happen to be writers belonging to a bygone era, the task is much more difficult: others have occupied the niches where they might (not 'should') have been and they cannot easily be dislodged from those toughest of all pedestals: handbooks of what is often called world literature and is, in practice, just as often limited to the literature of, say, Western Europe mainly (and by that I mean the 'main' literatures of Western Europe), the Americas and Russia. Not only is it difficult to dislodge the canonised figures of literature; it is just as difficult to add a new name to the hallowed list. There are all kinds of reasons for this, of course, and this is not the place to enumerate them, but I might just as well be aware of them, always.

Nearly every Flemish schoolchild has heard of Guido Gezelle; the trouble is that almost no other schoolchild anywhere else has. He is one of the 'also-rans' in terms of world literature, which means that his niche has been filled, by Hopkins, among others, and Mallarmé. Even within the boundaries of his own literature, Gezelle has two things going against him. The first is his language, the second his reputation. Gezelle was a Roman Catholic priest and a philologist. In his first capacity he could muster but scant enthusiasm for what he regarded as the language of Calvinism – that is, the standard Dutch of his time, spoken mainly by the lettered burghers of Amsterdam and taught in schools in the Kingdom of the Netherlands and in what is now Indonesia. In the second capacity he was eminently well suited to develop a language more or less his own, based on his native West Flemish dialect which, through some quirk of history, still has almost the same phonological system as Middle Dutch. It would be only a mild exaggeration to say that today about half of Gezelle's language is unintelligible to the man in the street in Amsterdam, and about a quarter to that man's Antwerp counterpart. No wonder his work does not quite achieve the effect I would tend to think it deserves.

Gezelle's reputation has been grossly distorted by anthologists in search of suitable material for use in literature classes in Catholic schools. As a result several of his none-too-brilliant pieces (his bishop even coaxed him to stoop to the level of propaganda once in a while) have been drilled into generations of schoolchildren, which has usually been enough to make them reject thyme, verse and stanza as soon as they managed to make their escape from the educational system. The truly revolutionary poet Gezelle (always in the linguistic-stylistic, never in the ideological sense) who singlehandedly scraped off a four-hundred-year rust from his native sub-language and experimented with *poésie pure* before the term was coined, is relatively unknown even in his own literary milieu.

The pragmatics of the Nightingale poem are, quite obviously, primarily phonetic. Gezelle experiments with sound (*de la musique avant Verlaine*) and tries to imitate the song of the nightingale in words. It is obvious that the semantic aspect of the poem is less important than its phonetic counterpart. The translation will have to strike a balance between the two aspects, but the phonetic will, where necessary, take precedence over the semantic. The most obvious examples are, in this respect, to be found in the stanzas beginning with 'Now piping fine' and 'And now his rhythm'. 'Piping' sounds like its Dutch/West Flemish counterpart, but does not really have the same semantic value, and the roof of the original has no thatched coat, which has been constructed in the translation for reason of assonance and metre. Similarly the rhythm does not bounce off notes in the original – Gezelle's imagery never got that surreal, and the pearls do not dance on marble ground. In fact, semantically speaking these two stanzas are pretty close to the worst possible translation. And yet I say this without batting an eyelid, first because it is the effect of the whole text that matters, and I can give back to semantics in other stanzas what I have to take from it in these; and second because I cannot let semantic considerations interrupt the rhythmic flow of the poem, nor counteract its sound-pattern. Speaking of sound-pattern, I have had to imagine what might be acceptable to the reader of the translation in 1980. Swinburne's stock is not generally high with the general public, and I have therefore thought it wiser to omit the rhyme (which, in previous attempts, tended to degenerate into doggerel) and to opt for some kind of assonance, each stanza being constructed roughly around a dominant sound, which is given by the semantic aspect and modifies it as the stanza unfolds. Do I therefore drag Gezelle kicking and screaming into the twentieth century? I do not think so. For one thing, it would be the worst kind of treason to translate a stylistic innovator into a kind of mock-Edwardian English verse (a translation of this type has actually been produced and is sold to unsuspecting tourists who, no wonder, are not exactly enthusiastic about Gezelle's literary potential); for another, it is the twentieth-century reader of English, and he alone, who decides whether Gezelle is ever going to 'make it' in English or not, and not the Dutch philologist who is able to give you the etymology and the exact pattern of derivation of all non-standard words in the poem. Here, too, I have opted for sound instead of sense, and for contemporary sound and sense over attempts at archaization – I do not believe Gezelle's cause would at all be served by translations with glossaries appended, or translations that would send the reader as often to the OED as the original would send him to a bilingual dictionary.

We should make it easy on ourselves – we translators – and calmly tell the world that total equivalence (the kind of thing that used to be clamoured for in handbooks) simply does not exist, and that the best we – and our readers – can hope for is some kind of optimal approximation. That is always possible, even if it has certainly not been achieved in the translation offered here. But that is my fault, not the fault of any language or any fateful concept of necessary untranslatability. I may not be good enough, but at least I am honest. I do not project my neuroses or my ideology into the text written by a country priest many years ago, and what I write about him will not much serve my personal advancement. I hope that what I translate may serve his. And after all this doctoring of the text, to make some final remarks, am I still brazen enough to maintain that translation can aspire to the status of a scientific activity? Certainly. Anybody who is qualified can compare my text with the text of the original, can see what I have done, and can accept it or reject it. We can argue about what I have done. I may be able to convince him or he me. I do not try to preach at him, or sweep him off his feet, or hit him over the head with truth and beauty. That is not my task. In the final analysis, I try to dispense knowledge – about Gezelle and about (his) poetry. The kind of knowledge that can aspire to the scientific – that can be checked, tested – but also the kind of knowledge that goes beyond the scientific may, in the end, be more important for the reader; but that is for him to decide. My job is done if I have succeeded in giving him the means to do so.

Waar zit die heldere zanger, dien	Where sits that limpid singer
ik hooren kan en zelden zien,	I can hear and seldom see
in 't loof geborgen	behind his screen of leaves
dees blijden Meidagmorgen?	this glad morning in May

Hij klinkt alom de vogels dood,
bij zijnder kelen wondergroot'
en felle slagen,
in bosschen en in hagen.

Waar zit hij? Neen, 'k en vind hem niet,
maar 'k hoore, 'k hoore, 'k hoore een lied
hem lustig weven:
het klettert in de dreven.

Zoo zit en zingt er menig man,
vroegmorgens op 't getouwe, om, van
goên drom te maken
langlijdend lijwaadlaken.

De wever zingt, zijn' webbe dreunt;
de la klabakt, 't getouwe dreunt;
en lijzig varen
de spoelen heen, in 't garen.

Zoo zit er, in den zomer zoel,
een, werpende, op den weverstoel
van groene blaren,
zijne duizendverwig garen.

Wat is hij? mensche of dier of wat?
Vol zoetheid, is 't een wierookvat,
daar Engelenhanden,
onzichtbaar, reuke in branden.

Wat is hij? 't Is een wekkerspel,
vol tanden fijn, vol snaren fel,
vol wakkere monden,
van sprekend goud, gebonden.

Hij is ... daar ik niet aan en kan,
een sparke viers, een boodschap van

He stuns the other birds
to silence with bold notes
that drop in wonder from his throat
in hedge and undergrowth.

Where is he? I can't find him but
I hear, I hear, I hear
the song of joy he weaves
it clatters down the streets.

Men sit like him and sing
before their looms when morning
comes and from good thread spin
long-lasting linseed-cloth.

The weaver sings, his frame shudders,
the shuttle keeps the beat,
the loom drones and the spools
move drawling through the woof.

So he sits in sultry Summer
and stretches his proud thread
of many colours on
the weaver's frame of leaves.

What is he? man or beast, joy
or sweet delight, a vessel
of incense where angels' hands
invisible burn many scents.

What is he? A clockwork toy
of fine teeth, fierce strings and
a dapper mouth all wrapped
in speech that sounds like gold.

He is ... what I can't reach,
a spark of fire, a message

veel hooger' daken	from roof's much higher than
als waarder menschen waken.	the boldest roof's of men.
Horkt! Langzaam, luide en lief getaald,	Listen! Slow and loud
hoe diep hij lust en leven haalt,	and lovely, a life, a zest
als uit de gronden	that sound as from the depths
van duizend orgelmonden!	of a thousand organ-mouths.
Nu piept hij fijn, nu roept hij luid';	Now piping fine, now screaming
en 't zijpzapt hem ter kelen uit,	loud it dribbles from his throat
lijk waterbellen	like waterbubbles rattling
die van de daken rellen.	down the roof's thatched coat.
Geteld, nu tokt zijn taalgetik,	And now his rhythm bounces
als ware 't op een marbelstik,	off each note – long necklaces
dat perelkransen	of pearls gone dancing off
van 't snoer gevallen, dansen.	their strings on marble sound.
Geen vogel of hij weet zijn lied,	A master of his voice
zijn' leise en al zijn stemgebied,	he knows to counterfeit
bij zijnder talen,	the lilt, the manner and
nauwkeurig af te malen.	the sweep of each bird's speech.
't En deert mij niet, hoe oud gedaagd,	An old man knows no envy:
dat hij den zangprijs henendraagt,	let him take the prize of song,
en, vogel schoone,	bird or beauty, and steal
mij rooft de dichterkroone!	the poet's crown from me.
Wat mensche en heeft u nooit verstaan,	For who will understand
noch al uw' rijkdom recht gedaan,	and treasure all the riches
o wondere tale	it holds, the marvel-tale
van koning Nachtegale!	of the sovereign nightingale.

PAUL VINCENT

CHRONOLOGY OF GEZELLE'S LIFE AND WORK

1830	Born Bruges, May
1846	College at Roeselare
1850–4	Theological studies at Bruges
1854	Ordained as priest
1854–60	Teaches at Roeselare
1858	*Dichtoefeningen* (Poetic Exercises)
	Kerkhofblommen (Churchyard Flowers)
1860	Director of English College in Bruges, teaches at Anglo-Belgian Seminary *Kleengedichtjens* (Short Poems)
1862	*Gedichten, gezangen en gebeden* (Poems, Songs and Prayers)
1881–95	Edits political weekly *'t Jaar 30*
1864	Chaplaincy of St Walburga, Bruges
1865–72	Editor-in-chief of cultural weekly *Rond den Heerd* (Round the Hearth)
1870–2	Edits *'t Jaar 70*
1871	Transferred to Kortrijk
1880	*Liederen, eerdichten et reliqua* (Songs, Odes et Reliqua)
1881	*Driemaal XXXIII kleengedichtjens* (Thrice XXXIII Short Poems)
1881–95	Edits *Loquela*, a periodical on West Flemish dialect
1886	Translates Longfellow's *Song of Hiawatha*
1887	*Tijdkrans* (Wreath of Time)
1888	*Rijmsnoer om en om het jaar* (Garland of Rhyme Round and Round the Year)
1899	Returns to Bruges, dies 27 November
1901	*Laatste gedichten* (Last Poems)

TEN VERSIONS OF 'O LIED'

O LIED

o Lied o Lied!
Gij helpt de smert
wanneer de rampen raken,
gij kunt, o Lied, de wonde in 't hert,
de wonde in 't hert vermaken!
o Lied, o Lied!
Gij laaft den dorst,
gij bluscht het brandend blaken,
gij kunt, o Lied, de drooge borst
en 't wee daarvan doen staken,
o Lied! o Lied,
het zwijgend nat
dat leekt nu langs mjjn kaken,
gij kunt het, en uw kunst is dat,
gij kunt het honing maken ...
o Lied! o Lied!

1860

A number of translators were asked either to produce a version of the above poem and comment briefly on their difficulties/strategies as translators, or to comment on an existing version. In one case, Christine D'haen's translation, published in her Guido Gezelle. Poems *(1971), p. 35, the translator was dissatisfied with the English rendering and let it be known that she did not wish it to be included here, despite the argument that discussion of why a particular version had 'failed' might in itself be illuminating. (PV)*

o Song! o Song!
You ease the smart
that's wrought by some disaster.
You take, o Song, the wounded heart,
and make the wound heal faster!
o Song, o Song!
You slake the thirst,
you quench the scorching fire,
you break, o Song, the arid worst
and make its pain retire,
o Song! o Song,
my silent tears
that fall now ever quicker,
you make – and now your Art appears–
You make them honey liquor ...
o Song! o Song!

Asked to contribute an English version of Gezelle's 'O Lied' at relatively short notice and at a time when I was preoccupied with other projects, my first inclination was to refuse outright. Looking at the poem, however, the first thing that sprang to mind was an alliterative, metrical, rhyming translation of the first stanza. This encouraged me to go on, and within minutes I had a fair working version of the second stanza as well. Suddenly there was no turning back. Bad luck for me, because the third stanza proved much less cooperative.

The coincidence of these first two stanzas falling into place also defined the translation tactics and stylistic features of the whole translation. I was locked into my instinctive approach. I maintained the original structure and regular metre and also its pattern of single and double rhymes. I felt forced to abandon the six-fold rhyme on '-aken', but another happy coincidence provided an English echo of the original in the many 'ache' sounds. I also opted for a mildly archaic vocabulary and usage. This seemed to suit the structure and content of the poem: more pronounced use of archaisms or dialect would run the risk of sounding absurd; overly modern language could clash with the old-fashioned style.

This was the context in which I began my struggle with the third and final stanza. What to rhyme with honey? Which part of the face lends itself to a double rhyme that ties in with tears and tasting? Temple or nostril? I do not think so. This is what I mean by the coincidental character of my translation tactics. If the third stanza had been first, I would have most likely resorted to a quite different approach. As it was, I tried hard to bend the poem to my structure. Ultimately I found solutions I can live with. Perhaps with more time I might have found better ones, but translations are like that, and poetry translations doubly so.

David Colmer

SONG!

O song! O song!
You soothe the smart
When grief comes back again
You can, O song, assuage the heart
And take away its pain.
O song! O song!
You slake my thirst,
You soothe my fevered brow,
You vivify my arid breast,
You banish all my woe
O song! O song!
When silent grief
Makes wet these cheeks of mine,
Then only you can bring relief,
Make honey from their brine.
O Song! O song!

I was drawn to this poem because of its double sentiment of sorrow (or dejection) and yet solace, no doubt a frequent experience for us all. Indeed I can feel the tears on the cheek and even see them on the page.

I did not, if I remember correctly, encounter great difficulty in my attempt at translation, partly because I am prepared to allow myself some freedom when I consider that the essence of a poem comes first and the pursuit of literal precision second. Inevitably, of course, line content will often not be parallel, and sentence structure must also often be different; see how in typical Flemish the infinitive *staken* is widely separated from its auxiliary and comes thus *after* its direct object. I have, I hope successfully, avoided inversions such as might not please in modern English poems.

I have not extinguished the flame of the eighth line, but perhaps the fevered brow will get by instead, even though the rhyme which it provides is only approximate. As for *brine*, I know it is not in the poem except by implication, but it does provide a rhyme. Even so, this is not a two-syllable rhyme as in the Flemish, but it indicates a frequent difficulty with translation, from either Flemish or German; in English so many sounded final e's and so many verb and noun inflections have been dropped from the pronunciation that I have decided not to despair if I do not often manage double rhymes.

Albert van Eyken

Oh song! Oh song!
You ease the pain
when disaster aims its dart
you, oh song, can mend again,
can mend the wounded heart.
Oh song! Oh song!
You assuage our thirst,
you quench the burning glow,
you, oh song, can surely nurse
the breast that used to flow.
Oh song! oh song!
The silent tears
That now drip down my cheek,
you – and this your art that cheers
can make them honey sweet ...
Oh song! oh song!

This note gives an account of the factors which played a part in determining the shape and wording of this English version of the Gezelle poem.

The translation does not capture the style and flavour of the Gezelle poem. By this I mean that because of my personal tastes, I decided not to use a regional or archaic kind of English. So 'gij', for example, was not rendered as 'thee' or 'thou', partly a reflection of this translator's lack of an active command of this style of English, but partly also because of the judgement that the translation could come close to pastiche, which I wanted to avoid. I also rejected the poetic or archaic word order that is found, for example, in some English translations of hymns from the mid nineteenth century, and which would have resembled Dutch structures more closely.

The starting-points for this translation were rhyme and metre on the one hand, and emotive force on the other. Although the rhyme scheme was preserved, full rhymes were not always possible, and in these cases assonance was used instead. In a similar way, the metre of the Flemish poem was reproduced in part, though the fourth line interrupts the iambic pattern with a trochaic one. This formal framework guided the translation of individual words and phrases, including the insertion of words such as 'cheers' and 'sweet' not present in the poem in Flemish. Besides addition, it also involved subtraction, with the loss of '*wee*' in line 10, and consequently of an emotive element.

Jane Fenoulhet

OH SONG!

Oh Song! Oh Song!
You ease the pain
and each misfortune's aching,
you can, oh Song, the heart's cruel chain,
the heart's cruel chain be breaking!

Oh Song! Oh Song!
You slake the thirst,
the raging blaze's raking,
you can, oh Song, the parched breast's curse
and sore distress be breaking.

Oh Song! Oh Song!
the silent bead
that down my cheek is quaking,
you can, oh Song, by art succeed
in sweetest honey making ...

Oh Song! Oh Song!

My initial reaction to 'O Lied! O Lied!' was 'Oh God!'. I think that is still my reaction. Three times arms are flung out in the grand gesture – and I am left with the feeling of a superabundance of form (some of it a teenie bit contrived?) and a dearth of content. (And in this case it seems valid to me to separate the two.)

Having established three stanzas of 4, 4, 7, 8, 7 + coda and a rhyme scheme ABCBC/ADCDC/AECEC/A, the main problem seems to me to be: If I retain all this as well as the set positions where phrases are repeated, I end up with six feminine C rhymes that are going to have to end in -ing. And that means putting verbs at the end of a sentence in a 'versifying' style I hate. It reminds me of homemade songs sung to known melodies at Danish parties and weddings – the 'Now we with joy this day are celebrating' sort of line.

And translation is reduced to a jigsaw puzzle, where only a few pieces are missing, but none of them fit. As a child I used to push them in a bit harder and hope. This is what I intend to do here, too. It is an admission of failure.

There have been few changes. Not because I rushed off a version, but because words like 'bane' are a pain in themselves. Here is the scaffolding:

Oh Song! Oh Song!
You x x x
x x x x x consonant +/eɪkɪŋ/,
you can, oh Song, x x x x
x x x x x consonant +/eɪkɪŋ]/.
The missing pieces were then rammed more or less into place.

John Irons

O SONG!

O Song! O Song!
You soothe the smart
When fortune strikes us low,
You can, o Song, bind up the heart
Which bleeds at a grievous blow.
O Song! O Song!
You slake the thirst,
you quell the fiery glow,
the breast, o Song, with dryness cursed
you calm, you calm its woe.
O Song! O Song!
Each silent bead
which down my cheeks doth flow
you can, o Song, transform to mead –
this art you also know!

The first job I do with poems is to read them through for general tone, structure, etc. It struck me as a fairly typical mid-nineteenth-century piece, not over-incisive in content (can a good sing-song really do all this?). Possibly meant to be set to music, in fact, rather than to be read.

The arrangement on the page hides the fact that the rhythm is that of the ballad: 4 beats – 3 beats – 4 beats – 3 beats, with a rhyme on the 3-beat lines. What makes it a bit more complex than your stock nineteenth-century ode is the rhyme scheme: the 4-beat lines also rhyme, and the same rhyme runs through all the 3-beat lines in the poem. Also the 3-beat rhymes are feminine and the other rhymes are masculine. But that's probably not something to worry about overmuch (it's probably due to the fact that a lot of Dutch sentences end in an infinitive, which almost always means a final unstressed -*en*).

Translating it was fun: I got stuck in with gusto. The general tone – coat-and-tails and evening gown round the mahogany piano and the aspidistra – sets the vocabulary: 'the smart / when fortune strikes us low', 'with dryness cursed', 'each silent bead / which down my cheeks doth flow'. With the first version, I went slightly over the top, translating 'gij' as 'thou' ('Thou sooth'st the smart'). This was vetoed, however, by my better half – who, besides being my native speaker informant, also acts as my quality controller.

The rhyme-scheme was mean: it took the best part of an afternoon just to get the set of six 3-beat rhymes. Somewhere along the way, this meant losing the parallelism of 'gij kunt' ('you can') in the fourth line of each stanza: I compensated for this by repeating 'o Song' in each fourth line instead. Similarly, I had to lose the blatant padding of 'de wonde in 't hert, / de wonde in 't hert vermaken', but managed to get some compensatory padding in the second stanza ('you calm, you calm its woe'). Of course, the rhyme scheme forces you into slight deviations from the original: 'wetness' becomes 'bead', 'honey' becomes 'mead', and so on. But I refuse to feel guilty about this. After all, it's often painfully obvious that original poets choose certain words only because they rhyme ('nat' and 'dat', for example), so why should not the translator be allowed the same privilege?

Francis R. Jones

o Song! o song!
The pain I feel
Whenever trials o'erwin me,
You can, o song, soothe hurt and heal
The wounded heart within me.
o Song! o song!
You quench the thirst
You quell the blazing reeling
You can, o song, restore the worst
Of pain in my parched feeling.
O Song! o song!
The tacit tears
That make my cheeks so runny
You have the power, as now appears
To turn them into honey,
o Song! o song

Questions of interpretation arise right from the start: in the title. This, with its lack of punctuation and its use of upper case throughout, gives no indication of the intention behind the refrain. Here there is punctuation, but there is also a consistent use of upper- and lower-case initials in 'Lied, lied'. The suggestion is surely that there is a transcendental Song and an immanent song: the Gift and what is given. This presents no problem to the translator, who can simply reproduce the typography of the original.

The translator is, however, immediately aware of the poem's unusual structure. Its two asymmetrical halves pivot symmetrically about the median. The form of the stanza is tied into the refrain held firmly at the centre. This means that the form contributes essentially to the meaning, and the translation must reflect this form as faithfully as possible.

This raises the basic question: if a choice has to be made between exact rendering, rhyme or rhythm, which should be sacrificed? In trying to retain the alternation between male and female rhymes as well as the syllabic rhythm of the original, I have taken some liberties with the literal meaning.

Peter King

SONG!

Song! Song!
You lessen the pain
whenever disaster tries us,
you tell us, O Song, the heart is wounded in vain,
wounded in vain, you advise us!
Song! Song!
You slake our thirst,
you dowse the blaze that fries us,
you irrigate, O Song, the driest breast,
undo the knot that ties us.
Song! Song!
The silent tear
creeping down our cheek supplies us
with honey: so be here, be near
and by your art surprise us –
Song! Song!

The main problem is the rhyme scheme. It would be easy to give a close rendering without taking it into account, but I felt that the chiming effects were very much a part of the attraction of the poem, and so some attempt should be made to reproduce them.

Edwin Morgan

a) **O LYRIC SONG**

O lyric song!
You ease the smart
when trouble has its seasons,
your power upon the wounded heart
brings solace to its lesions!
O lyric song!
Song that will salve,
quencher where thirst is regent,
you can that burning drought dissolve
and drive out torment's legions.
O lyric song,
I feel a damp
witness of stealthy weeping
that, such your canniness, you can
transform to honey's sweetness ...
O song! O song!

b) **SONG**

   O song, song, song!
You tend the smart
 inflamed by trouble's flailing
and so enwind the wounded heart
you turn away its ailing!
   O song, O song!
  When parched with thirst
 you douse its fiery dealing,
you can, O song, undo the worst
drought has to harrow feeling.
   O song, O song,
  this damp that leaks
over my cheeks distilling
can, as the candid silence speaks,
turn honey by your willing ...
   O lyric song!

The initial decision as to which aspects of a text's dynamic to highlight has a profound effect on how a translation will turn out. In fact, I had to make two radically different versions of this poem, with differing aims in mind.

Gezelle's poem itself, regarded simply as a poem, is neither profound nor original. It is chiefly a vehicle for lyricism of a rather simple kind, its metre undeviatingly iambic; such metaphors as it has are traditional, apart from the final conceit. The word-music is more sophisticated, especially the repeating feminine rhyme and the wordplay on 'kunt' and 'kunst'. The way the sense progresses is most interesting of all. Mental pain is alleviated by song; the pain is caused by longing or deprivation, a drought song quenches; this quenching is accomplished by the release of tears, made sweet by the lyrical act. The poem is in fact describing its own effect.

I only got to know the poem well by working on the first version and, at the end, wondering where I had gone wrong. My first impression had been that meaning hardly mattered; it was merely the vehicle through which Gezelle demonstrated his lyrical mastery. I made the conscious decision to produce a paraphrase round which to weave a music of my own, a formal equivalent employing internal, near, off and pararhyme. In fact, the version owes more to Basil Bunting than to Guido Gezelle. Because I had in mind such Elizabethan set pieces as those on night and sleep ('that knits up the ravelled sleeve of care'), the metaphors verge on the Baroque. It is a travesty of the original.

The next move was to look at the poem in its historical perspective. In 1860 Gezelle was still suffering from the emotional crisis of the year before, following the loss of a favourite student and, besides, had been dismissed from the professorship of poetry at the seminary where he was working. An adequate reason to be down in the mouth! Nevertheless, his approach is impersonal and generalised. Of more importance is the reason for the poem's simplicity, its lack of original sentiment. Poems like it may be two a penny in English and many another major European language – but they were not in Flemish, owing to the chequered history of the Belgian territories. Gezelle is having to pioneer a style and a language to fit it. In the light of this, the sophisticated procedures of 'O Lyric Song' are out of place.

'Song' attempts a version that is simpler and closer to the original. Two approaches I rejected at the outset. Flemish forms are at a minimum in this and would not justify a dialect rendering. Scots would be too radical; Yorkshire dialect offers the attractive possibility of a familiar second-person singular ('tha') but is not really supple enough. On the other hand, I had once suggested in a review that the Victorian boudoir syntax of the Claes and D'haen versions (*The Evening and the Rose,* revised edition, Antwerp, 1989) produced a useful distancing. They underline the fact that what we are reading belongs to the nineteenth century. It would have been valid in this case, too, but I could not bear the thought of using it myself (apart from one inverted verse form in my first version).

How to handle the repeated 'O lied' presented a problem in both versions. There is a modulation from back vowel to front in the Dutch not present in the English grunt of 'O song'. Dutch liquid and dental consonants give way to English sibilant and nasal which, to my ear, have a dying fall. For that reason I only used this particular repetition at the end of 'O Lyric Song'. I chose the phrase of the title because at least the vowel modulation is represented and gives the better initiatory lift to the poem; also because it underlines the poem's main interest, lyrical effect rather than the act of singing or listening. It was not an alternative open to the more literal second version, but the objection to repeating 'O song' remained. What came to the rescue was the memory of the triple repetition in the first line of 'Careless Love'. Its intensity grips the attention. Hopefully it might do the same for Gezelle's sister song!

Beyond that, the rhymes in 'Song' are regular. Although it was not possible to preserve the repeated feminine rhyme, each stanzaic section has a pure rhyme and overall they are near rhymes of each other. There are also a few metrical deviations in the form of inverted first feet. Unvarying iambic is a Germanic practice (listen to any high school student reciting), the deadly boredom of which I suspect Dutch use of feminine rhyme is meant to alleviate. English practice requires variation.

I am not satisfied even with the second version. It still falls short of Gezelle's simplicity and some of his patterns of repetition. On the page, they strike me as rather fiddly. Sung, they might be more effective, and producing a translated text for singing would bring other priorities to the fore.

Yann Lovelock

O SONG!

O Song,
thou makest less the grief
of calamity sore afflicting,
canst, Song, to the sore heart bring relief,
to the wounded heart's distressing!
O Song, O Song!
thou quenchest parching thirst,
dampenest fire's fierce scorching,
replenishest, Song, the empty breast
in milkless sorrow paining.
O Song! O Song,
those wordless tears that start
now down my cheeks a-flowing,
thou canst – for such is thy sure art –
canst honey soon be making ...
O Song! O Song!

To translate is to refract, even to fracture. What follows is *post f(r)actum*. The poem effectively contains three similar 'quatrains', referred to below without qualifying quotation marks.

TECHNICAL
Three constraints made competitive play.

1. *gij* (= thou/you) occurs on no fewer than seven occasions, all line-initial. In each quatrain Gezelle uses once or twice one or both of the structures *gij* + finite verb and *gij* + modal verb *kunnen* + (end-positioned) infinitive. In l. 15 *gij* + *kunnen* (+ – here – pronominal direct object of l. 14 is repeated), syntactic tension resulting from both this and from the separation by parenthetical 'en uw kunst is dat' of the two occurences of 'gij kunt het'. In striving to preserve the second person, I used (second person) morphs in *-est* and *-st* in each quatrain to 'carry' the person, *them* having been pronominally established in a previous line. *Thou* was, however, revived in l. 15 in order to stabilise the sense and to prelude the climactic tension of ll. 15–16.

2. End rhyme. Using *-ing* to render unstressed *-en* seems reasonable enough, but *-en* figures here in more parts of speech than *-ing* (can) in English: some compensatory lexical duplication ensued ('sore afflicting', 'wounded ... distressing', 'sorrow paining'). Even using a different consonant phoneme to maintain equivalence or the *rime riche* in *-ken* would have led to a surfeit of verbal contortion. The persistent stressed end rhyme in *-(t)*, present also in final 'Lied' and mirrored frequently elsewhere, is emulated in the second – with 'thirst' approximating to 'breast' – and third quatrains, but 'grief/relief' in the first one proved too enticing!

3. Gezelle's broadly iambic metre was maintained, in eluding the four stresses in ll. 4, 9 and 14. However, the addition of one iamb in the first line of each quatrain meant that ll. 2, 7 and 12 no longer had the same number of iambs (two) as the four 'O Lied / O Lied' lines – a loss.

REGISTER
We know that this poem, like at least two, possibly three, others in *Gedichten* ... was written for Gezelle's Roeselare pupil Polydor Demonie, in *c.* 1860 aged 15 or 16 (see *Verzameld dichtwerk*, vol. 2, 56 and 52, 64, 69). Is the 'Lied' being addressed in our poem a *pars pro toto* metaphor for a musical pupil? After all, in Bizet's opera Carmen(cita) both song and person. Such proximity of priest and pupil might justify *you* for *gij*. On the other hand,

Gezelle's time-hallowed lexis and prosody in most of the poem inclined me to archaic *thou*, fitting for matters serious, intimate – and poetic. Moreover, I sometimes even expanded the hymn-echoing tone of much of the original, partly also, despite Gezelle's concision, to avoid too abrupt a rendering (e.g. in the first quatrain 'calamity sore afflicting', 'sweet relief', 'wounded heart's distressing').

EQUIVALENCE?

The original's parenthesis 'en uw kunst is dat' is alas rather clumsy, with its filler 'en' in the feeble sequence 'het, en uw, and its inelegant end rhyme in 'dat': but *should* one have sought to improve? Even clumsier is the collocation of 'de drooge borst' (= the dry breast) with 'doen staken' (= make [to] cease), even allowing for 'de drooge borst' plus ''t wee' being a hendiadys. Furthermore, the *meaning* of 'de drooge borst' is elusive: is emotional or pulmonary incapacity (tubercular perhaps) meant? Or the reading chosen? To the latter I was persuaded by the 'fluid' context of the final quatrain. So I opted for the verb 'replenishes!' – biblically soothing – with both literal and figurative meaning in order to make more startling the adjective 'milkless' in 1.10, which itself adumbrates the even greater but amazingly positive and sensual verbal impact of the miraculous 'honey'.

A cautionary tale: if each quatrain enacts a transformation from hurting to healing – more intense in the second, at its climax in the third quatrain – then 'tears' are licensed to come before 'honey' *et sic translatum est*. Yet suppose 'het zwijgend nat' (l. 12)', (*nat* = fluid, liquid, moisture, water, wet) indicates incipient drops of *mother's milk*, the *product* of l. 9's restorative action. In that case the second and final quatrains – and we have observed oddness in the latter – refer to a *single* process of transformation rather than to parallel transformations, and a different rendering of the phrase is required.

Self-evidently, any interpretation should embrace the poem's also being a paean to the ultimate finding of *poetic* utterance. In the 'mother's milk' reading, 'incipient drops' would then suggest the *ébauche* of such verbalisation, 'honey' – in all readings – creative achievement. The poem becomes poetological, referring to its own genesis. 'Maak je de borst maar nat', one might conclude, before again venturing into a land of *such* milk and honey.

Michael Rigelsford

POEMS AND TRANSLATIONS

1848

DE MANDELBEKE (fragment)

... daar weleer de schoone Mandel,
in heur kronkelenden wandel,
van waar heure bronne spruit
tot waar zij heur water spuit
in de temme Leiebaren,
vrij van kommer en gevaren,
door de schoone groene streek
vloog ...! De snelle Mandelbeek,
vloog door menig groene weide,
die ze kuste en lekte en vleide;
menig derde vissel schoot ...
Maar dit alles is verdwenen!
Droever dagen zijn verschenen;
't Mandelwater schiet nu vuil
door den watermolen kuil.
Niet een vogel komt er kwelen,
niet een ande 'n komt er spelen,
Waar zij heure baren giet
en besmette dampen schiet.
Zelfs mag daar geen visch meer dertelen
of 't om hem dood te spertelen;
niet een lammeken bedorst,
durft er koelen zijne borst;
noch geen zwaluw in heur plasschen
wil sneeuwwit hertje wasschen,
al dat leeft, het schuwt de kreek,
en 't veracht de slavenbeek.
Daarom zucht ik, daarom steen ik,
daarom, neêrgebogen, ween ik ...

1848

THE MANDEL STREAM (fragment)

Here once the lovely Mandel Stream
used to flow, with winding course
from where her source began, to where
she sent her waters into the docile
River Lys. Here she used to swiftly
flow, free from care and danger,
through the green and beauteous fields ...
and so through many a pasture land,
which caressing, coaxing, she rendered fertile ...
But that is over now;
sad days have fallen on the Mandel Stream,
which pours foul waters
from out the water wheel.
No bird comes there to trill his song,
no duckling comes to play,
where turgid waters run,
exhaling impure vapours.
No longer can a fish dart there,
except to hasten to its doom:
no thirsty lambkin there can
cool its parchd throat, nor
dare the swallow wash its snow-white
breast with plashing in the river.
All that lives avoids the creek,
and despises the enslaved stream.
That is why I sigh, why I groan,
that is why I weep ...

(MS)

1852

AANROEPINGE

Blomkes, lieve blomkes zoet,
die uw hertjes open doet
bij den eerst morgengroet,
    schittert in mijn zangen;

Beekske, klappend beekske klaar,
dat uw blanke waterbaar
over 't zand laat varen, dààr,
    vaart ook in mijn zangen;

Hellemende nachtegaal,
gij, gij spreekt de dichtertaal,
laat uw bosschen, komt eenmaal
    helmen in mijn zangen;

Windtje, dat op 't water sliert,
of al door de bosschen tiert,
als u God den teugel viert,
    wappert in mijn zangen;

Donder, die al dondren komt,
die in d'holde wolken bromt,
die en mensche en dier verstomt,
    dondert in mijn zangen:

Blomme, beke, nachtegaal,
windenstemme, dondertaal,
blanke bleeke manestraal,
    looft God in mijn zangen!

1852

REPLY IN VERSES

Flowers, beloved flowers sweet,
let your little hearts now beat
as you the early morning greet;
and glitter in my verses.

Softly babbling rivulet
whose summer-sunlit shallows fret
babble in my verses.

Peal at evening, nightingale
from your thicket in the dale,
bring to me your poet's tale,
tell it me in verses.

Winds that play upon the lake,
or whisper in the willow brake,
or bid the mighty forest shake,
join me in my verses.

Thunder, rolling thunder, come,
sound in heaven like a drum,
strike me for a moment dumb,
echo in my verses.

Rivulet, flower and singing bird,
wind and thunder, seen or heard!
How the heart in me is stirred,
praising God in verses!

(AE)

1855

BOODSCHAP VAN DE VOGELS EN ANDERE OPGEZETTE DIEREN

Hoort en neemt ons tale in achte,
kinders van het pluimgeslachte,
liefste broeders, groot en kleen,
die daar floddert onder een.
Gij die al de krinkelwegen
in het hemelrijk gelegen
weet te vinden in uw vlucht
door de licht doorvlogen lucht,
gij die, diepe in 't loof gedoken
of in 't lommerwelf beloken
van het dik bewassen woud,
kunstig daar uw nestjes bouwt,
en in 't duiksel van de blaren
pluimkes, mos en wollenharen
samen tot een wiegske vlecht
en daar al uw hope inlegt,
vol van moederlijk verlangen,
vol van vreugde en blijde zangen:
d'hope van 't geheel geslacht,
van der bonten vederdracht! –
– eikes schoonste schoon der wereld,
eikes, blinkende en bepereld
en gespot rondom de schaal,
met het bleuzendste coraal:
geel we, bruine, hemelblauwe,
fijn gevlekte, grijze, grauwe,
dicht gewolkte in't heldergroen,
van geen mensche na te doen;
zwart geplekt en wit gespegeld,
dicht gesijperd of getegeld,
eikes naar den rechten zin,
schoon van buiten, goed valt bin'. –

1855

MESSAGE FROM THE BIRDS AND OTHER STUFFED ANIMALS

Listen now to our advice,
you members of the feathered race,
brothers, sisters, great and small,
pinion-flappers one and all,
you who look to travel by
the unseen pathways of the sky,
and lean upon the yielding air,
skilful pilots everywhere;
or you love the thickets best
where you may build yourselves a nest
of feathers, wool and mosses made,
hidden in a leafy shade,
your little dwelling closely knit,
where you upon your hopes may sit
or, full of bird solicitiude,
forage for your gaping brood,
where mid the leaves and flutterings
it seems the very woodland sings
in united celebration
of the coming generation;
eggs all shiny, or bepearled,
garnished round about with specks,
coated thick with coral flecks,
yellow, brown or heaven blue,
gay-bedecked in every hue,
thickly washed in brilliant green,
none prettier have you ever seen;
darkly russet-covered quite,
and not forgetting black or white;
eggs one must judge genuine,
pretty outside, sound within.
Happy, happy nightingale,

Blijde blijde nachtegale,
eerlijk en van schoonder tale,
die zoo helder en zoo zacht
hellemt in den stillen nacht;
broeder leewerk, hemelwekker,
zevenzanger, bietjestekker,
slaande kwakkel ende vink;
en gij ook al, koddig ding,
dat, met't steertjen opgesteken,
en het koofke recht gestreken,
kruipt en klavert op den stam
van den eeke stijf en stram;
vogelkes uit allen lande,
vogelkes van allen stande,
vogels kort en vogels lang,
vogels met of zonder zang,
vogels groot en vogels kleene,
vogels hoog en leeg te beene,
met een steert gelijk nen pauw,
met een steertje scherp en nauw,
een van lange lange pluimen,
of waa 't eentje van twee duimen;
hebt een snavel, recht of krom,
hebt een baard of geen daarom,
en een rooden kam benevens,
met een paar roo'lillen tevens,
met een truizel bovenop,
en een koofken op den kop:
Gij moogt hoog, kort, lang, smal, breed zijn,
gij moogt alleszins gekleed zijn,
in 't fluweel of in 't satijn
of in 't donzig hermelijn;
zijden kleeren of katoenen,
donker blauwe oft helder groene:
grimselzwart of hagelblank,
kleur van hoog- of leegen rang:
goud, dat onder 't groene kronkelt,

teller of eve's fairytale,
you whose limpid notes take flight
through the creeping shades of night;
brother-skylark, heaven-watcher,
darting, twisting, fleet bee-catcher,
quail, or finch with flirting wing,
and you too, you funny thing,
who, with tiny tail upright,
and your crest erect and tight,
creep and clamber up the bark
of the oak-tree rough and stark;
birds from over lands and sea,
birds of high and low degree,
birds built short and others long,
birds that know, or know not, song,
birds full fat and birds right small,
birds minute or long-shank tall;
with a kind of peacock tail,
or maybe one lone feather frail,
maybe just a lanky plume
or tiny as a baby's thumb;
with a straight of crooked beak,
with, or sans, a beard on cheek,
with a red comb on the crown,
with two bright wattles hanging down,
or a tuft upon the head,
or an eye ringed round with red;
tall, short, long or in between,
in varied garb you may be seen,
made of velvet or sateen
or yet of downy eremine;
clothes of silk or more subdued,
with shiny green or blue imbued,
chimney-black or snowy white,
colours pale or dazzle-bright;
with gold a-glitter through the green
or green upon a golden sheen,

groen, waar brandend goud op vonkelt,
bruin gebronzeld, lijk metaal,
rood als een robinenstraal;
fijn geringeld en geregeld,
en gespikkeld en gespegeld,
zoet verdwijnend afgeleid
't een in 't ander weggevleid
en ten nieten uit verbleekend;
kleur, zo stekende afgeteekend
en zo net vaneen geplekt,
en zoo lief geschaaljedekt,
dat geen een van al de menschen
beter zoude doen of wenschen ...
Zanggebroeders uit het woud,
met uw talen duizendvoud:
Gij, die kwinkt en gij, die kwedelt,
gij, die schuifelt en die vedelt,
gij, die neuriet, gij die tiert,
gij, die piept en tiereliert,
gij, die wistelt die teutert,
gij, die knotert en die kneutert,
gij, die wispelt en die fluit,
gij, die tjiept en tureluit,
gij, die tatert en die kwettert,
gij, die klapt en lacht en schettert,
vezelt, orgelt, zingt en speelt,
lispelt, ritselt, tjelpt en kweelt,
gij, die kwinkelt lijk de vinken,
en alom gaat slaan en klinken,
met uw bekken, licht en los,
dat het kettert in den bosch:
fluiters, zangers ende slagers,
ermers, kriepers ofte klagers;
vogels die, op Gods geleê,
hier ten lande of over zee,
jaagt dat uwe vieren zoeven,
achter 't gone u mag behoeven,

brazen brown as might be metal,
or red as any red rose petal,
bright with wavy stripes and spots,
or finer lines and smaller dots,
one into the other running,
interspersed by nature's cunning,
or shading modestly away
into lustrous sober grey;
or as sharply set apart
as in the skilful tiler's art –
No! better, I assure you,
Than anything a man can do!
All you tuneful woodland throng
with your languages of song,
you who click and you who warble,
you who squawk or gently treble,
you who hum and you who coo,
you who pipe or tooraloo,
you who whistle or who stutter,
you who chatter, you who mutter,
you who whisper or who flute,
you who cheep or boldly hoot,
you who tattle or who swear,
you who yell or laugh or blare,
gossip, boom, or chant or play,
lisp or rustle, chirp or bray,
you who rather choke than sing,
you who yell and you who ring,
you whose voices sweet and clear
fill the woodlands far and near,
birds who sing with joy – or shout
of things they wish to moan about;
birds who at the Lord's command
travel over sea and land;
you who flutter after food,
whatever titbit may seem good,
be it crust or dainty dish,

achter 't gone uw voedsel is,
kooren, vruchten, vleesch of visch,
vliegen, motten, andre kerven,
al wat gij maar kunt verwerven.
Gij die, op uw lange been',
diep in 't slijk zit, met uw teen',
g'reed staat, met den hals gestopen,
tot dat iets komt uitgekropen,
dat gij seffens vastesnakt,
zoo gij menig puitje pakt,
dat, van uit zijn vuile dijken,
zeer voorzichtig eens kwam kijken
wie dat't was die daar zoo stond
op zijn erfelijken grond;
nauwlijks is de puit nog boven
of uw bek, omleeg gestoven,
lijk een vleiel op het kaf,
stekt den puit zijn lenden af
Gij ook, dievig muschgebroedsel,
levende op eens anders voedsel,
gij, die elk ende een verwijt
met hetgeen gij zelve zijt.
Vogels zoet of fel van aarde,
alle vogels van der aarde,
hoe gewapend, hoe gereed,
vogels, hoe gij ook al heet,
wilt alhier uw gangen stieren,
komt en maant ook andre dieren,
dat ze komen neerstig aan
naar ons paradijs gegaan! –
- Sichten dat wij hier geraakten,
en, God lof, de dood gesmaakten,
ai 't is heel een ander ding,
bij dat 't van te vooren ging!
't Was van 's morgens, alle dagen,
dóór de winden, dóór de vlagen
er de kop was uit de vlerk,

corn, or fruit, or flesh or fish,
flies or moths or other kind
of insect that may please your mind.
You who stand with bean-stick legs,
toes sunk in the river dregs,
dagger drawn, and moveless there,
waiting creatures that may dare
come forth; you heron on the watch
for any tasty bit to catch
as when perhaps a juicy frog
from underneath a sodden log
peeps to see who comes to roam
here in his ancestral home,
and straight you stab into the muck –
alas! Poor frog is out of luck,
for scarcely has he moved a limb
before your beak dismembers him!
And you! Thieving sparrow breed,
careless of each other's need,
who think your neighbours are to blame
when yourselves do just the same.
However fierce or tame you be,
birds of low or high degree,
birds of peace or birds of war,
birds whatever stock you are,
wing your air-paths hitherwards.
Here you'll find not only birds,
creatures who have humbly come
to this our paradisal home.
Here, both bird and quadruped,
we find ourselves together – dead!
For matters here are not the same
as in the days before we came!
Then we lived, through every hour,
come the wind or come the shower,
scarce the head from under wing
a life of constant labouring.

altijd arbeid, altijd werk;
Honger zat ons achter d' hielen,
Honger wilde ons al vernielen,
zoo daar een verzuimen do'st
van te werken voor den kost.
Des was 't altijd stelen, rooven,
op den akker, in de schooven:
al waar dat er iets bestond
dat was mage of borst gezond.
Honger zelfs kost ons bedwingen
menig een ter dood te bringen;
wee voor al 't onnoozel bloed
dat de honger storten doet!
Daarbij mochten wij, o dwazen,
in rust en vreden azen,
maar daar schrikte ons altijd iets,
zelfs al was 't een enkle niets.
't Is dat wij nog niet en wisten,
dat de looze jagerslisten
en het sterven zelfs ons leidt
tot de schoone onsterflijkheid.
Ja, wij dachten 't was ons schade,
maar het was ons een genade
dat een jagers tooverroer,
naar een welgemikten loer,
met een weêrlicht op ons afging,
dat het heen en weder paf ging.
Nooit en zullen 't wij verstaan:
maar als 't roer was afgegaan,
kwam daar iets in ons gevlogen
at den honger heeft verjogen,
at hij nooit meer weêr en kwam,
met zijn herdelooze vlam;
en de slaap, die ons voordezen,
altijd vluchtig plag te wezen,
hield ons, veertien dagen lang,
in het zoetste rustbed wang.

Hunger followed us about,
hunger sought to snuff us out
if we should ever dare to shirk
or never-ending load of work.
Oft we had to pick and steal
to win ourselves a skimpy meal
of any remnants that might stop
the craving of an empty crop.
A gnawing hunger often brought
many lives, also, to nought;
woe to such as, seeking food,
were caught by foes who spilt their blood!
Thus through our dread of sudden death
we never could draw peaceful breath.
In our breasts we always fear
though no real danger might be near,
for indeed we never knew
what some cunning foe might do,
and any moment we might be
conveyed into eternity!
But what seemed pity in our eyes
was yet a blessing in disguise.
Thus if a huntsman hunting came
and took a very careful aim,
then a clap of sound rang out
and woke the echoes round about:
understand it we did not,
but when there came a sudden shot
something struck one in the breast
and set one's hunger pangs to rest;
henceforth the old familiar pain
never would come back again,
and quiet sleep, which hitherto
so many of us never knew,
now could be enjoyed until
any bird had had its fill.
What happened in our bosoms then

Wat ons toen van menschenhanden
wierd gedaan in de ingewanden
dat en spreekt geen vogeltaal,
zelfs al waar 't een nachtegaal.
Maar 't ontwekken ... 't was 't herleven!
Zoo die slaap ons had begeven,
Zag ons krystalinen oog
't alderwonderste vertoog:
rondom, in den blauwen schemel
van den schoonen voglenhemel
zaten wij onsterfelijk,
met nog menige, ons gelijk.
Andren, die wij nooit en zagen,
en zoo schoone pluimen dragen
dat geen een van ons alhier
reeken kan aan zulken zwier,
zaten daar ook, vol gezondheid,
in hun kunstgemeten rondheid,
groot- en schoonder als weleer,
edeldrachtig en vol eer.
Alle veedte is hier vervlogen,
hier wordt nimmermeer bedrogen
de arme vogel, noch verklikt,
noch bij nachte half dood geschrikt.
Vogel ende wezel mede,
leven hier in rust en vrede,
ziftende, naar hun gemak,
huns getween op éénen tak.
Onze onsterfelijke voeten
moeten in geen slijk meer wroeten,
noch geen koude of hitte uitstaan,
om den nooddruft na te gaan:
spijs, die alle spijzen weerd is,
altijd nieuw en nooit verteerd is,
spijs, die, ongeëten, voedt,
spijs, die sterfloos voort doet leven,
wordt den vooglen hier gegeven

at the hands of hunting men,
of that no bird can tell the tale,
not even could the nightingale.
But when from sleep at last we woke
things were altered at a stroke,
and here, before our crystal eyes
a most incredible surprise!
For unawares we birds had come
to this our paradisal home,
and here we sat no more to die
with many like us sitting by;
many whom we'd never seen
and of such a gaudy sheen
as none of our acquaintance might
ever hope to rival quite.
We sat there having had our fill
through the taxidermist's skill,
looking healthy, if not more
sleek and handsome than before.
Here you will not find a cheat,
here there is no more deceit.
No bird gets sneaked on, nor by night
driven to extremes of fright.
Bird-and-weasel struggles cease,
both together live in peace,
sitting side by side at ease
on branches in the happy trees.
Our immortal toes are stuck
no longer into mire and muck;
no longer do our exposed feet
have to suffer cold or heat:
now food that is the very tops,
food that always fills our crops,
food that, unconsumed, still feeds
sufficiently our daily needs,
food which keeps us living on,
food from stomach never gone,

en hun buik met iet verzaad
dat daar nooit meer uit en gaat.
Hier is 't werken afgeropen,
't jagen, 't stelen end het stropen,
al dat ruize of moeite kost,
daarvan is men hier verlost.
Rusten is ons bezig hou'en,
rusten en malkaar aanschouwen
en beschouwd zijn en bezien
van die beste jonge liên,
die studenten, vol van goedheid,
vol van eedle grootgemoedheid,
die ons eertijds maakten schuw
maar die wij beminnen nu;
want ze minnen ons en maken
dat geen leed ons kan genaken,
ziekte, droef- of kwalijkheid,
hier in 's vogels zaligheid.
Al 't geluk dat wij genieten
komt van hun en komt voor nieten,
komt dat 't alle wicht en maat
verre weg te boven gaat:
zoodat, sichten wij hierboven
rusten in onz' Hemelhoven,
wij al wierden stom daarvan,
noch geen een die 't spreken kan,
of zijn wonderinge toogen,
of zijn hertlijk mededoogen
voor ons arrem broedertal,
nog geboeid in 's werelds dal.
Maar, bij overdaad van goedheid,
helpen zij onze onbevroedheid,
- zeggen zij, in onzen naam,
waartoe wij zijn onbekwaam: –
- Broeders, in 't gevang der wereld
nog aan 't leven vastgespereld
en gevangen, luistert hier:

food an everlasting store,
gizzard stuffed for ever more.
Here it is the end of work
here there is no more to irk,
her at last we have been freed
of every quarrel, toil or need.
Now we are released from bother,
now we just survey each other,
spending all our easeful days
basking in the curious gaze
of students loved by all of us,
so many most magnanimous,
who at one time caused us fear –
but now we love to have them near;
for they attend us with such care,
no other guardians can compare;
here is no sickness or distress
in this our birdland's blessedness.
Here our joy, as you may see,
comes from them and comes for free,
so that it measures far above
what others may be thinking of.
To represent our heavenly dwelling
there are not words enough for telling;
we are just dumbfounded quite,
nor can we describe aright
all the miracles we see,
nor describe such sympathy
for our other poor compeers
still fettered in the vale of tears.
By their excess of goodness
we are helped in our simplicity;
they say on our behalf just what
we for our part now cannot:
Brothers in the world retained,
still to earth's misfortune chained,
listen now to what we say:

PAUL VINCENT

laat uw nutteloozen zwier,
laat de bosschen en de hagen
uwen zin niet meer behagen;
keert uw lang bedwellemde oog
eindlijk toch eens naar omhoog:
wilt hetgeen gij placht te duchten,
wilt het sterven niet meer vluchten,
vliegt den jager in 't gemoet,
dat hij u de gunste doet,
met zijn tooverroer, te zenden
eenig zaad in uwe lenden,
zaad des levens dat de dood
zal doen vluchten uit uw schoot.
Komt! Wij reeken onze vlerken,
komt toch! Wilt niet langer werken
leeft met ons in weelde en vreugd
en in altijd jonge jeugd.
Laat uw levensdraad verfijnen,
laat uw namen verlatijnen,
laat een oog van krystalijn
uw vernieuwd gezichte zijn.
Komt, en laat u weêr verjongen,
al het oude zij verdrongen,
wascht het morzig aardsche slijk
van uw voet gezwindelijk,
en met kloeke vederslagen,
rap den lichtweg ingeslagen
die de dood voor ingang heeft,
maar die leedt waar dat men leeft.
Menschen, tot ons heil geschapen,
grijpt 't onsterflijkmakend wapen,
't zij ons broederen lief of leed,
stelt u tot het jagen g'reed:
g' hebt de onsterflijkheid in handen,
zendt ze hun in de ingewanden!
Van den lichaamsvrechte ontdaan,
van der dood weêr opgestaan,

leave your profitless display,
leave the hedgerow and the wood,
give up all these things for good;
turn your long-distracted eye
finally to life on high:
choose to flee life's troubles sore,
flee the fear of death no more.
Fly to meet the sportsman who
may do something good for you:
let him sow within your gut
a scattering of leaden shot,
seed that means new life and rest,
drives death itself out of your breast.
Come! We stretch out wings to you.
Seek for no more work to do.
Live with us in luxury,
stay young henceforth eternally.
Live a life more civilised,
have your species latinised.
Let artificial eyes enhance
the brightness of your countenance!
Come! Win again a youthful presence,
oust all the signs of sad senescence!
Wash away all messy slick
from off your feet – and double quick!
Spread a ready-beating wing
and with eager effort fling
yourselves at once along the path
to life beyond the door of death –
and man, whose shotgun is our friend,
ensure for them a lasting end.
Some brothers may still have their doubt,
but be prepared to seek them out;
bring an end to their painful lot
with just a burst of leaden shot!
Delivered from their life of pain
and risen from the dead again,

PAUL VINCENT

zendt ze, na kortstondig slapen,
hier geheel in 't nieuw geschapen.
Gij ook, die naar 't lieve land,
waar gij gingt aan moeders hand,
wederom uw stap gaat richten,
wilt ons broederen gaan berichten,
roept en dwingt ze, uit haag en heg,
toogt hun vriendelijk den weg;
zegt het hun op alle wijzen:
Komt ten voglenparadijzen,
waar gij eeuwig leven zult,
heel onsterflijk,–opgevuld. –

DE AVERULLE EN DE BLOMME

Daar zat ne keer een Averulle
    En lekte met nen zom,
        zom, zom,
den dauw van op de blaren,
die klaar bedreupeld waren
    lijk met nen dreupel rom,
        rom, rom.

Wanneer zij fraai gedronken had,
    zoo vloog ze scheef en krom,
        rom, rom,
al neuzlen en half dronken,
tot waar de kleêrkes blonken
    van eene schoone blom,
        lom, lom.

De blomme die ze kommen zag
    En viel niet al te dom,
        dom, dom,

after sleep's brief interlude,
display them here with life renewed!
You students too, so soon to be
back home among your family,
go out at once among the birds,
address them in your own wise words;
at copse and hedge without delay,
in friendly manner show the way;
persuade our brothers to be wise
and join our avian paradise,
where our taxidermists will
skilfully their bellies fill!

(AE)

THE COCKCHAFER AND THE FLOWER

There once sat a cockchafer
and licked up with a yum,
yum, yum,
the dew from off the petals
that seemed all sprinkled over
as if with drops of rum,
rum, rum.

When it had drunk its fill then,
it flew all daft and dumb,
dumb, dumb,
sniffing and half-drunk now
to where the petals glistened
of a chrysanthemum,
mum, mum.

The flower saw it coming
and did not act so dumb,
dumb, dumb,

maar riep zoo, loos van zinnen:
'Hei, Kobbe, kom mij spinnen
een kobbenet rondom,
om, om.'
En Kobbe, die was seffens g'reed,
en steld' heur pootjes krom,
rom, rom.
Zij spon heur looze netten
om heur daarin te zetten,
en zat daar stille en stom,
tom, tom.

En als de Rulle kwam nabij
geflodderd, krom, en slom,
lom, lom,
zoo is ze in 't net gevlogen,
en deerlijk uitgezogen,
ofschoon zij jankte: 'Zom
zom zom!'

De looze blomme loech ermee,
die looze booze blom,
lom, lom,
eilaas! Zoo menig jonkher
wordt uitgezogen pronker,
om eene schoone blom,
dom! Dom!

Uit het Duitsch.

*

Timpe, tompe, terelink,
Vliegt van hier na Derelijk,
vliegt van hier na Rompelschee,
koper kop en stalen tee;

but cried out, craftily,
'Hey, spider, come and spin me
a web around my tum,
tum, tum.'
The spider was soon ready,
and bent its legs and bum,
bum, bum;
it spun its web with cunning
and sat right in the middle
and stayed there still and mum,
mum, mum.

The chafer fluttered slowly
and nearer it did come,
come, come.
Entangled in the cobweb,
it was sucked quite empty,
though it lamented, 'Hum,
hum, hum!'

The crafty flower laughed then,
the sly chrysanthemum,
mum, mum,
alas! So many suitors
are sucked dry in pursuit of
a fine chrysanthemum,
dumb, dumb!

From the German

(PV)

*

Hyder iddle diddle dum,
Fly from here to Middleton,
Fly from here to Bockenfield,
Copper-knob and toe of steel;

wilt hij op zijn been niet staan;
'k moet er met de zwepe op slaan:
Timpe, tompe, terelink.

1857

HET SCHRIJVERKE (Gyrinus natans)

O krinklende winklende waterding,
    met 't zwarte kabotseken aan,
wat zie ik toch geren uw kopke flink
    al schrijven op 't waterke gaan!
Gij leeft en gij roert en gij loopt zoo snel,
    Al zie 'k u noch arrem noch been;
gij wendt en gij weet uwen weg zoo wel,
    al zie 'k u geen ooge, geen één.
Wat waart, of wat zijt, of wat zult gij zijn?
    Verklaar het en zeg het mij, toe!
Wat zijt gij toch, blinkende knopke fijn,
    Dat nimmer van schrijven zijt moe?
Gij loopt over 't spegelend water klaar,
    En 't water niet meer en verroert
Dan of het een gladdige windje waar,
    Dat stille over 't waterke voert
O Schrijverkes, schrijverkes, zegt mij dan, –
    Met twintigen zijt gij en meer,
En is er geen een die 't mij zeggen kan: -
    Wat schrijft en wat schrijft gij zoo zeer?
Gij schrijft en het staat in 't water niet,
    gij schrijft, en 't is uit en 't is weg;
geen Christen en weet er wat dat bediedt:
    och, schrijverke, zeg het mij, zeg!
Zijn 't visselkes daar ge van schrijven moet?
    Zijn 't kruidekes daar ge van schrijft?

If his pins refuse to budge,
Whip him soundly, then he'll trudge,
Hyder iddle diddle dum.

(YL)

1857

THE WATTER-SCRIEVER[i] (Gyrinus natans)

O croinklie crowlie watter-thingie,
croont wi beret sae bleck,
it's gret yer wee heid's ay sae springie
as ye scrieve tae sick effeck!
Ye leeve an ye muive en ye gang sae swith,[ii]
though wi fient[iii] an erm or leg;
ye birl[iv] wi sic an eident[v] pith,[vi]
though withoot an ee – whit a geg![vii]
Whit wiz ye, whit ur ye, whit'll ye be?
Wull ye no spell it oot, ma dear?
Wi yer braw wee skinklin[viii] heid ajee,[ix]
whit maks ye scrieve and steir?[x]
Ye traivel owre the glessy watter
wi nae mair runkle therr
nor whit a fuff o win micht shatter,
ye pitter-patterer!
O scrievers, scrievers spik tae me then,
twinty o ye, nae doot,
tell me, wan o ye, jist wan, ye ken,
what scrievers ur scrievin aboot?
Ye scrieve, and the watter losses it,
ye scrieve sae gleg,[xi] an it's gane;
nae Christian comes up an endosses it:
och scriever, ye tell me nane!
Ye scrieve aboot wee fush, zat it?
Ye're a scriever o the sproats?

Zijn 't keikes of bladtjes of blomkes zoet,
    of 't water, waarop dat gij drijft?
Zijn 't vogelkes, kwietlende klachtgepiep,
    of is 'et het blauwe gewelf,
dat onder en boven u blinkt, zoo diep,
    of is 't u, schrijverken, zelf?
En 't krinklende, winklende water-ding,
    met het zwarte kapoteken aan,
het stelde en rechtte zijne oorkes flink,
    en bleef daar een stondeke staan:
'Wij schrijven,' zoo sprak het, 'al krinklen
    af het gene onze Meester, weleer,
ons makend en leerend, te schrijven gaf,
    een lesse, niet min nochte meer;
wij schrijven, en kunt gij die lesse toch
    niet lezen, en zijt gij zoo bot?
Wij schrijven, herschrijven en schrijven nóg,
    den heiligen Name van God!'

Scrieve stanes, leafs, flooers, ye're at it?
Scrieve whaur yer boady floats?
Scrieve burds that chirm[xii] an cheep and peep,
or the bew[xiii] that's owre awthing
ablow,[xiv] abune,[xv] leamin[xvi] sae deep –
or is it yersel ye're scrieving?
An the croinklie crowlie watter-thingie
croont wi beret sae bleck
heezed[xvii] up its lugs with a bra flingie
an pit its birl oan the sneck:[xviii]
'We're scrievin,' it sayed, 'in oor croinklie way
whitever oor Maister telt us
oor makar, ooe dominie, tae scrieve an tae say,
the wan bit lear[xix] he selt us:
we scrieve an kin je no jaloose,[xx]
or ur ye thick as a brod?[xxi]
We scrieve, re-scrieve, scrieve richt roose[xxii]
the haly name o God!

(EM)

NOTES

i writer
ii quickly
iii never a
iv whirl
v diligent
vi strength
vii trick
viii gleaming
ix cocked to one side
x stir
xi fast

xii chirp
xiii blue
xiv below
xv above
xvi gleaming
xvii raised
xviii latch
xix lesson
xx suspect
xxi board
xxii excitedly

O 't RUISCHEN VAN HET RANKE RIET

O! 't ruischen van het ranke riet!
o wist ik toch uw droevig lied!
wanneer de wind voorbij u voert
en buigend uwe halmen roert,
gij buigt, ootmoedig nijgend, neêr,
staat op en buigt ootmoedig weêr,
en zingt al buigen 't droevig lied,
dat ik bemin, o ranke riet!

O! 't ruischen van het ranke riet!
Hoe dikwijls dikwijls zat ik niet
nabij den stillen waterboord
alleen en van geen mensch gestoord,
en lonkte 't rimplend water na,
en sloeg uw zwakke stafjes ga,
en luisterde op het lieve lied,
dat gij mij zongt, o ruischend riet!

O! 't ruischen van het ranke riet!
Hoe menig mensch aanschouwt u niet
en hoort uw' zingend' harmonij,
doch luistert niet en gaat voorbij!
voorbij alwaar hem 't herte jaagt,
voorbij waar klinkend goud hem plaagt;
maar uw geluid verstaat hij niet,
o mijn beminde ruischend riet!
Nochtans, o ruischend ranke riet,
Uw stem is zoo verachtlijk niet!

OH! THE RUSTLING OF THE SLENDER REED!

The rushes swayed beside a murmuring stream
Homer, *Iliad* XVIII, 576

Oh! the rustling of the slender reed!
I would I knew thy mournful song!
Whenever the wind doth pass thee by
And gently breathe upon thy stem,
Thou bendest, humbly bowing down,
Then risest up to humbly bow again
And sing, whilst bending, that sad song
That I so love, O slender reed!

Oh! the rustling of the slender reed!
How many a time have I sat down
Beside the silent water's edge
Alone and undisturbed by man,
And gazed at the rippling waves.
And touched thy tender stem
Whilst listening to that dear song
Thou used to sing, O rustling reed!

Oh! the rustling of the slender reed!
How many a man perceives thee not,
Nor listens to thy harmonious sounds
He listens not and passes on
To where his heart enticeth him,
To where the sound of chinking gold allures;
But thy sweet sound he understandeth not,
Oh my beloved rustling reed!
And yet thou slender rustling reed
Thy voice is not to be despised

God schiep den stroom, God schiep uw stam,
God zeide: 'Waait!... en 't windtje kwam,
en 't windtje woei, en wabberde om uw stam,
die op en neder klom!
God luisterde ... en uw droevig lied
behaagde God, o ruischend riet!

O neen toch, ranke ruischend riet,
mijn ziel misacht uw tale niet;
mijn ziel, die van den zeleven God
't gevoel ontving, op zijn gebod,
't gevoel dat uw geruisch verstaat,
wanneer gij op en neder gaat:
o neen, o neen toch, ranke riet,
mijn ziel misacht uw tale niet!

O! 't ruischen van het ranke riet
weêrgalleme in mijn droevig lied,
en klagend kome 't voor uw voet,
Gij, die ons beiden leven doet!
o Gij, die zelf de kranke taal
bemint van een en rieten staal,
verwerp toch ook mijn klachte niet:
ik! Arme, kranke, klagend riet!

AAN DE LEEUWERKE IN DE LUCHT

aan R. Willaert

Mijn beminde Grijslawerke,
    lieve zangster ende zoet,
die, op uw bedauwde vlerke,
    met uw altijd reinen voet

God made the stream, God made thy stem,
God said, "Oh, come thou little breeze" –
And the breeze came and fluttered round
Thy stem, making it tise, then bend.
God listened, and thy mournful song
Was pleasing to Him, rustling reed!

Ah no, thou slender rustling reed,
My soul despiseth not thy song:
My soul that from God Himself
At His command received the gift
To understand thy rustling sound
Whenever thou dost rise or bend:
Oh no, oh no, thou slender reed,
My soul despiseth not thy song!

Oh! the rustling of the slender reed.
Let it resound in my sad song,
And lamenting come before Thy Throne,
O Thou Who gavest life to both!,
Thou, Who lovest the mournful song
Of a tapering reed, reject Thou not
My sad complaint, for I, too, am
 A poor, lamenting, sickly reed!

(MS)

TO THE LARK IN THE SKY

to R. Willaert

Dear Skylark, you so grey of hue,
dearest singer oh so sweet,
who, on wings all drenched with dew
with your pure untainted feet,

de aarde stoot, en, afgevlogen
    hooger dan mijn ooge draagt,
daar, in d' hemelblauwe bogen,
    daar aan God uw klachte klaagt;
daar waar gij den dag ziet breken,
    wandlende op de wolkenbaan,
schouwende in de gulden streken
    éér de zonne is opgestaan,
zingende op heur eerste lonken
    uw verrukte vogeltaal,
drinkende met lange dronken
    d' aldereersten morgensttraal:
'k heb u dikwijls nagekeken,
    vruchtloos, in uw hooge vlucht,
ende mijne ziel geleken
    bij de leeuwerke in de lucht.
Spant, o ziele, spant uw veren
    veerdig tot de hemelvaart,
wilt niet langer hier verteren:
    op, geliefde, hemel waard!
Schuwt al wat u kan bezwaren,
    werpt het, schudt het, slaat het af.
wilt geen van die krachten sparen
    die God zelf, o ziele, u gaf!
Laat ze, die deze aarde minnen,
    lustig hunne wegen gaan,
achter 't geen waarmeê de zinnen.
    de ijdle zinnen zijn voldaan,-
menig vogel wroet zijn leven
    lang, en lustig, in het slijk,
gij, moet met den leeuwerk zweven,
    hooge in 't blauwe hemelrijk.
Daar zult ge over hille en dalen
    schouwen in den gulden Oost,
baden in de morgenstralen,
    in die zee van hope en troost!

shoot up from earth, and flying high,
higher than the eye can see
there in the blue vaults of the sky
make complaint to the Deity;
there, where you see the day is dawning,
travelling the cloudy ways,
survey the golden streaks of morning
before the risen sun's ablaze,
singing at the first faint peep
your exultant avian lay,
drinking in with draughts so deep
the very earliest morning ray:
after you I've often stared
in vain to see you soar so high,
and my soul I have compared
to the skylark in the sky.
Spread, o soul, extend your wings,
ready for the heavenward flight,
dally not with earthly things:
up, my dear one, seek the light!
Shun all that weighs so heavily,
cast it, shake it, brush it off you,
don't spare strength reluctantly
that God himself has given to you!
Let those who love this earth below
blithely go upon their way;
beyond whate'er the sense delights,
the idle sense's vain array,
many birds spend long days and nights,
happily wallowing in the mire,
you must with the skylark soar,
high to heaven you must aspire.
There, o'er hill and valley floor
you see East's beaming heliotrope,
bathing in the morning beams
in that sea of solace, hope!

Troost voor 't altijd weenend herte,
    dat maar immer vreugde 'n vraagt,
troost voor de onverzoenbre smerte
    die daar altijd, altijd knaagt:
knaagt tot als wanneer gij rusten,
    rusten zult in 't heilgenot
an die zee, die zonder kusten,
    zonder gronden is, in God!
Leeuwerke in de hemelstreken
    blijft gij nimmer, nimmer lang,
maar gij moet het lied afbreken
    van uw blijden morgen zang;
gij moet weêr op de aarde dalen,
    eens verstooten met den voet,
moet alhier het voedsel halen
    dat u, arme, leven doet;
maar, mijn ziel, wanneer uw vlerken
    eens, na lang verleden tijd,
losgaan ende mogen werken,
    en gij vrij van 't lichaam zijt,
dan, o dan! zoo vliege ik henen,
    snelder vlieg ik op de vlucht,
dan gij, Leeuwerk, ooit verdwenen
    zijt in 't diepen van de lucht.
Dan, o dan! zoo vliege ik hoog en
    hooger, in mijn hemeltocht,
dan gij mij den weg kunt toogen,
    Leeuwerke in de blauwe locht.
Dan, o dan! zoo keere ik nimmer,
    nimmer, nimmer, nimmer weer,
maar ik blijve, schouwend immer
    immer in het gulden meer
van dien Oceaan van Goedheid,
    van dien Oosterdageraad,
die, wie eens genoot zijn zoetheid,
    nimmer, nimmer keeren laat!

Balm for heart's ever-flowing tears
when joy is what it's longing for,
balm when grief never disappears
that gnaws and gnaws for ever more:
gnaws until at last you reach
pure salvation's holy joy,
and in that sea that has no beach
and no bottom, God's peace enjoy!
Lark, up in the heaven's bounds,
you never stay up there for long,
but must halt the tuneful sounds
of Your joyous morning song;
you must descend to earth again
that just now you left behind,
must search for food upon the plain,
so you may live on what you find;
but, my soul, when your two wings
one day, when many years have past,
begin to move and make strong swings,
and, free of body's weight at last,
then, oh then I'll fly away,
faster soar with all my might
than you, Lark, speed at break of day
into heaven's dizzy height.
Then, oh then! I'll take the air,
go higher, in my heavenly flight
than you can guide me through the sky,
skylark, in the azure there.
Then, oh then! return I'll never,
never, ever, ever more,
but will stay and look forever
on that gold sea without a shore
of that great Ocean full of Good,
of that dawning eastern dome,
and none who've tasted its sweet food,
can ever, ever go back home!

PAUL VINCENT

Dan, o dan! zoo zing ik lange en
   langer als 't u is gegund;
zoeter klinken mijne zangen,
   dan gij, Leeuwerk, zingen kunt.
Zoeter als de klokkegalmen,
   die, vermenglende in 't getuit
van de meziegolven, walmen
   's avonds als het avond luidt;
langer als 't gezang der winden,
   die, aan 't spelen onder 't riet,
daar de schrale snaren vinden
   van hun ruischend morgenlied;
zoeter als 't gelui der schellen
   toen 't al klinkklankt ondereen
van de koeien, die hun bellen
   kluttren, klinken, ende weên;
hooger als de hemelbollen
   die in eenige eenigheid
stralend door de ruimte rollen,
   in de oneindige eeuwigheid!

1858

IK DROOME ALREÊ

Ik droome alreê van u, mijn kind,
En van de blijde dagen, de dagen,
   Dat samen wij, en welgezind,
   Vliegt dagen vliegt voorbij gezwind,
     Ons lief en leed gaan dragen.

Ik droome alreê van u, mijn kind,
Noch late ik mij gelegen, gelegen
   Aan dat aardsch en bitter smaakt,
   Dat 't lijf en 't lijf alleene raakt,
     En daar de geest kan tegen.

Then, oh then! I'll sing so long,
longer than you, lark, are allowed;
much sweeter still will be my song
than those you, skylark, sing aloud.
Sweeter than the bells that chime
and mingle with the rushing round
as the swarms of midges climb
at evening when the vespers sound;
longer than the soft breeze sings
which when among the reeds it plays
and finds there the same scanty strings
it used to voice its morning lays;
sweeter than the sound of cattle
when each bell that dangles plays
and all the creatures gently rattle
the bell and ring it as they graze;
higher than the spheres on high
that in awesome solitude
roll resplendent through the sky
with eternal-life imbued!

(PV)

1858

I DREAM E'EN NOW

I dream e'en now of you, my child,
of happy days when we two will
together and with tempers mild –
pass days, pass days in tempo wild –
we'll share good times and ill.
I dream e'en now of you, my child,
and shall not be content, content
with earthly tastes that I detect
that feed but the body's element,
and that the spirit will reject.

Ik droome alreê van u, mijn kind,
Gij hebt hem doorgestreden, gestreden
   Den nacht dien 's vijands booze hand
   Gespreid had om 't beloofde land:
     Gij zijt er in getreden.

Ik droome alreê van u, mijn kind,
En, ga ik langs de straten, de straten
   Daar heemlijk in mijn herte weunt
   't gedacht, daar al mijn hope op steunt
     God zal u mij toch laten.

EEN BONKE KEERZEN KIND

aan Eugene Van Oye

Een bonke keerzen kind!
Een bonke keerzen kind,
   gegroeid in den glans
   en 't goudene licht
     des zomers!
Vol spannende zap,
   vol zoet,
   vol zuur,
  vol zijpelende zap,
   vol zoetheid!
Ze blonken aan den stamme,
ze spraken waar ze stonden:
  'Plukt ons, plukt ons,
    plukt ons,
  plukt en laaft uwen dorst,
  rijpe zijn wij en schoone! '
   Neigend hongen ze,
    zwinkelend
    in de wind,

I dream e'en now of you, my child;
you've fought on through now, fought on through
the night that the devil's evil hand
had used to shroud the promised land:
it has admitted you.

I dream e'en now of you, my child,
and walk the streets, walk through and through,
since in my secret soul abides
the thought on which my sole hope rides:
that God will grant me you.

(PV)

A BUNCH OF CHERRIES, CHILD

to Eugène van Oye

A bunch of cherries child!
A bunch of cherries child
grown in the gleam
and golden light
of summer!
Full of springing sap
full of sweet
full of sour,
full of seeping sap
full of sweetness!
They glistened on the stem,
they said from where they hung:
'Pick us, pick us,
pick us,
pick and slake your thirst,
we are ripe and fair!'
Bending, they hung
swaying
in the wind,

den lauwen wind
des zomers.
'Plukt ons, plukt ons,
plukt ons!'
riepen ze en ik plukte ze
en ze woegen zoo zwaar;
de zegen des Heeren woeg op hen.
Neemt en dankt Hem
die ze gemaakt heeft,
die ze deed worden,
dankt Hem, dankt Hem,
dankt Hem!
Kijkt naar den Hemel,
Daar is Hij,
daar is,
God!
De oogen omhooge,
gelijk den vogel
die drinkt
en 't schuldeloos hoofdeke om-
hooge heft,
dankt hem, dankt Hem ...,
dankt Hem!
Trouw als 't arreme dier,
trouw als 't loof en de vruchten,
trouw als 't blommeke,
trouw als
't zandeken onder den voet,
bedankt Hem!
o Geniet, 't is zoo zoet
eene vrucht te genieten die
rijpe is,
en vreugd en dank
te voelen rijzen in het herte!
Leert de tale die spreekt
uit monden duizende, en altijd

the tepid wind
of summer.
'Pick us, pick us,
pick us!'
they cried and I picked them
and they weighed so heavy
the blessing of the Lord weighed upon them.
Take and thank Him
who made them,
who created them,
Thank Him, thank Him,
thank Him!
Look towards Heaven,
there He is, there is
God!
With eyes on high,
like the bird
that drinks
and lifts its innocent head
skywards,
thank Him, thank Him ...
thank Him,
As faithful as the poor beast,
as leaves and fruit,
as faithful as the flower,
as faithful as
the sand underfoot,
thank Him!
O enjoy, it's so sweet, so sweet
to enjoy a fruit that
is ripe,
and to feel joy and thanks
swell in your heart!
Learn the language that speaks
from a thousand mouths, and forever

              roept: 'Den Heere zij
                        dank:
    dank om het leven
    dank om het licht,
dank om het licht en het leven,
dank om de lucht en het licht
en het zien en het hooren
                      en al!
    Dank zij den Heere!
    Een bonke keerzen kind,
    een gloeiende bonke ... be-
        dankt Hem!

DIEN AVOND EN DIE ROOZE

aan den voorgaande

'k Heb menig uur bij u
    gesleten en genoten,
en nooit heeft een uur met u
    me een enklen stond verdroten.
'k Heb menig blom voor u
    gelezen en geschonken,
en lijke een bie, met u, met u,
    er honing uit gedronken;
maar nooit een uur zoo lief met u,
    zoo lang zij duren koste,
maar nooit een uur zoo droef om u,
    wanneer ik scheiden moste,
als de uur wanneer ik dicht bij u,
    dien avond, neêrgezeten,
u spreken hoorde en sprak tot u
    wat onze zielen weten.
Noch nooit een blom zoo schoon, van u
    Gezocht, geplukt, gelezen,

calls: 'Thanks be to the Lord:
thanks for life,
thanks for light,
thanks for light and for life,
thanks for sky and for light
and for seeing and hearing
and all!
Thanks be to the Lord!
A bunch of cherries child,
A gleaming bunch ... O
thank Him!

(JH)

THAT EVENING AND THAT ROSE

to the same

Oh, many and many an hour with you
I've passed the time with pleasure.
And never has one hour with you
Been less to me than treasure.
Oh, many and many a flower for you
To offer you I've plucked
And like a bee, with you, with you
Its honey I sucked.
But never an hour so dear with you
As long as it could stay,
And never an hour so sad for you
When I must go away,
As the hour when I came close to you
That evening, and sat down
And heard you speak and spoke to you
Of all our souls had known,
And never a flower was plucked by you
So beautiful to see
As the one that shone that night on you

Als die *dien avond* blonk op u,
    En mocht de mijne wezen!
Ofschoon, zoowel voor mij als u,
    wie zal it kwaad genezen? –
een uur bij mij, een uur bij u,
    niet lang een roos mocht wezen,
toch lang bewaart, dit zeg ik u,
    't en ware ik 't al verloze,
mijn hert drie dierbre beelden: U
    DIEN AVOND – en – DIE ROOZE!

IN DE BLANKE LONKEN

In de blanke lonken
    Van de maan
Zat ik neergezonken
    Langs de baan
En ik schouwde verre
    Met mijn oog
Schouwde naar een sterre
    Daar omhoog
En de sterre beefde en
    Lonkte op mij 't alsof ze leefde
en lonkte zij
en ik zelve beefde en
    lonkte op haar
peizend dat ik leefde
    nauwlijks maar
peisde dat ik daar zat
    daar onhoog
waar die sterre klaar zat
    voor mijn oog
dat ik hoorde weemlen
    ongehoord
't zingen van de Heemlen
    altijd voort

And soon might come to me.
Although for me as well as you –
Oh, who can cure this wrong? –
An hour with me, an hour with you
Is not an hour for long
And though for me and though for you
So dear a flower we chose,
A rose, be it even a rose from you,
Remains not long a rose.
I keep three well loved pictures: you,
That evening, and that rose.

(CS)

IN THE WHITE MOON WINKING

In the white moon winking
with a ray
I sat down while sinking
on my way
And I gazed far there
with my eye
gazed upon a star there
standing high.
And the star while quivering winked at me
looking like a living winking she
And myself while shivering winked at her
thinking I was living
scarce astir

thought that I was sitting
there on high
where that star was glittering
to my eye
and I heard in choiring
harmony
Heaven's awe-inspiring
symphony

spreken hoorde ik engelen
    tot malkaar
en hun stemmen mengelen
    altegaar
'ik zag de hemelbollen
    op en neer
voor de voeten rolen
    van den Heer
't zand en loopt zoo dicht niet
    uit het glas
't glas en loopt zoo licht niet
    of zoo ras

ZILVERBLANKE ZWANEN

Zilverblanke zwanen, 'k groete u
'k groete u met den groet des dichters
met eens menschen groet gebroederen
die gebroeders, die gezusters
ziet in u en kinders van den
God die alles schiep dat iets is,
Zwanen twee beminde vrienden
Komt en wilt van mij gegroet zijn
Zilverblanke zwanen 'k groete u

Elpen vaten in den spiegel
's waters en 't krystaal hier herwezend
dat uw blanke schoonheid weergeeft
borst en borst tweevoudig afbeeldt
zoo van boven, zoo beneden
dat gij tweelings de een aan de ander
schijnt gegroeid en tweemaal een zijt
de eene omleege en de ander op waard.
Zilverblanke zwanen 'k groete u.

angels I heard singing
each to all
with their voices mingling
in one call
saw the spheres revolving
part and meet
orbs of Heaven rolling
near God's feet
sand runs not so tightly
from the glass
glass will not so lightly let
it pass.

(PC/CD)

SILVERY WHITE SWANS

Silvery white swans, I greet you,
greet you with a poet's greeting,
with a human greeting, brothers,
that sees brothers and sees sisters
in you and children of the
God who made all that is living.
Swans, you two much-loved companions,
come to me and let me greet you,

Ivory vessels in the mirror,
repeated in the glassy water
that reflects your snow-white beauty,
breast and breast depicted twofold,
once above, and once below it,
so you two just seem to grow
together and are twice one swan,
one goes downwards, one goes upwards.
Silvery white swans, I greet you.

(PV)

RAMMENTATI

Aan Domenico de' Pisani

'Oh! open the door to me, oh!' BURNS
Rammentati, onthoudt 'et wel,
de wereld is een zee, oh!
met baren, rotsen, winden fel
en nog al ander wee, oh!
Men geeft u wel
voor reisgezel
't genoegzijn en 't beheer, oh!
van al dat kan
de ziekte ervan
verzachten end' het zeer, oh!
Betrouw ze niet:
geen kort verdriet
maar wel een korte vreugd, oh!
alzoo gewis
de wereld is;
vol al dat niet en deugt, oh!
Maar, moet gij, en
ontwijdert men
u ver van mij verschee'n, oh!
dan, gaat, mijn kind,
voortaan hier gansch alleen, oh!
Wij scheiden met
dit laatst gebed:
maakt dat ik u nog zie, oh!...
onthoudt 'et wel,
mijn kind, vaart wel:
Rammentati, ... Addio! ...

RAMMENTATI

to Domenico de' Pisani

'Oh! open the door to me, oh!' BURNS

Rammentati, remember well,
the world, it is a sea, O!
with waves and wind and shipwreck fell,
and all that worse may be, O!
Can men bestow,
as forth you go,
the power to sustain, O!
the ills that may
come your way
and soften all their pain, O!
No! trust them not
that pain is short,
for shorter may be joy, O!
Remember well,
the world is full
of forces that destroy, O!
If fate should then,
or fellow-men,
keep you and me apart, O!
then go, my son,
and leave me lone,
with sorrow in my heart, O!
But first we'll share
a final prayer
that I see you again, O!
Remember well,
and fare you well,
Rammentati! ... Addio!

(AE)

1859

'T ER VIEL 'NE KEER ...

(*Herinnering aan Beethoven's Septuor*)

't Er viel 'ne keer een bladtjen op
    het water
't Er lag 'ne keer een bladtjen op
    het water
En vloeien op het bladtje dei
    het water
En wentelen winkelwentelen
    in 't water
Want 't bladtje was geworden lijk
    het water
Zoo plooibaar en zoo vloeibaar als
    het water
Zoo lijzig en zoo leutig als
    het water
Zoo rap was 't en gezwindig als
    het water
Zoo rompelend en zoo rimpelend
    als water
Zoo lag 't gevallen bladtjen op
    het water
En m' ha' gezeid het bladtjen ende
    'et water
't En was niet 't een een bladtje en 't an-
    der water
Maar water was het bladtje en 't blad-
    tje water
En 't viel ne keer een bladtjen op
    het water
Als 't water liep het bladtje liep
    Als 't water

1859

A LITTLE LEAF ONCE FLUTTERED ...

(Remembering Beethoven's Septet)

A little leaf once fluttered down
to t' watter
A little leaf once floated down
to t' watter
And flowing onto t' little leaf
cam' t' watter
And it were flowing, t' little leaf,
on t' watter
And theer it twirled and swirled about
i' t' watter
For now that leaf were well-nigh t' same
as watter
And theer it mickle-trickled just
like watter
And theer it dandle-dawdled just
like watter
And theer it skittle-scuttled just
like watter
And theer it ripple-ruffled just
like watter
That little ligging fallen leaf
on t' watter
Until tha could ha' said that t' leaf
and t' watter
Weren't one of 'em a leaf and t' oth-
er watter
But t' watter now were leaf, and t' leaf
were watter
A little leaf once fluttered down
to t' watter
When t' watter flowed, t' leaf flowed and all.

Bleef staan, het bladtje stond daar op
    het water
En rees het water 't bladtje rees
    en 't water
En daalde niet of 't bladtje daalde
    en 't bladtje
En dei niet of 't bladtje dei 't
    in 't water
Zoo viel der eens een bladtjen op
    het water
En blauw was 't aan den Hemel end'
    in 't water
En blauw en blank en groene blonk
    Het water
En 't bladtje loech en lachen dei
    het water
Maar 't bladtje en wa' geen bladtje neen
    En 't water
En was nie' méér als 't bladtjen ook
    geen water
Mijn ziele was dat bladtjen: en
    dat water? -
Het klinken van twee harpen wa'
    dat water
En blinkend in de blauwte en in
    dat water
Zoo lag ik in den Hemel van
    dat water
Den blauwen blijden Hemel van
    dat water!
En 't viel ne keer een bladtjen op
    het water
En 't lag ne keer een bladtjen op
    Het water.

When t' watter
Were still, then t' leaf lay just as still
on t' watter
When t' watter rose, t' leaf rose along
wi' t' watter
When t' watter fell, t' leaf fell as sharp
as t' watter
What t' watter did, t' leaf did and all
i' t' watter
This leaf it fluttered any road
to t' watter
And t' sky were blue and it were blue
i' t' watter
One glistening gleam o' blue and green
were t' watter
And t' leaf it laughed and wi' it laughed
all t' watter
But t' leaf it weren't no leaf now, it
were watter
And it were nobbut leaf, were all
that watter
That little leaf, it were my soul:
and t' watter?
A ringing o' two harps it were,
that watter
And glist'ning i' that gleaming blue
o' t' watter
I lay in Heaven in a sky
o' watter
In Heaven's blissful blue in all
that watter
A little leaf once fluttered down
to t' watter
A little leaf once floated down
to t' watter

(FJ)

WIE ZIJT GIJ

aan Hendrik van Doorne van Poucke

Wie zijt gij, pinkelend sterrenheer,
    dat aan de hemel staat?
Zijt gij de kroon van God den Heer,
    Zijn diamantsieraad?
Zijt gij de wachters, trouw en goed,
    die zijnen throon bewaart?
Zijt gij het zand waarop zijn voet
    al wandelen henenvaart?
Dient gij aan zielen duizendvoud
    tot woning en verblijf?
Zijt gij uit goud – of wat? – gebouwd
    en welk is uw bedrijf?
'k En weet niet ... en. Hoe kleen
    op dezen wereldbol,
een zandeken, een punteken,
    in 's hemels wijd heelal,
'k benijde u niet, o sterren daar,
    't wat gij zijt of doet,
ik beneide u niet, al hebbe ik maar
    mijn armen JEZUS zoet!
Zijn tabernakel bouwt Hij niet
    noch zijnen zetel zal
hij zetten in het stergebied,
    maar in dit tranendaal:
In Bethlehem, in Nazareth ...
    in Roomen, overal ...
hier heeft Hij zijnen throon gezet,
    hier in dit tranendal!

WHAT ARE YOU?

to Hendrik van Doorne van Poucke

What are you, shining starry horde
who fill the firmament?
Are you the crown of God the Lord,
his diamond ornament?
Are you the watchers true and tried
who guard his kingly seat?
Are You the sand spread far and wide
beneath his royal feet?
Are You the destined dwelling-place
of many thousand blest?
Are You the holy home in space
where all the saints find rest?
What then of my own nothingness
in this my earthly home?
A grain of sand, a spot – or less –
beneath the heavens' dome.
And yet I do not envy you,
whatever you may be,
For why indeed, why should I do,
with Jesus close to me?
He builds his tabernacle here,
as in the starry skies,
He rules us men and holds us dear
throughout this vale of sighs,
To Bethlehem he chose to come;
here he has set his reign,
Here he has made his royal home;
Here he shall come again.

(AE)

IK MISSE U

aan een afwezenden vriend

Ik misse waar ik henenvaar
   of waar ik henenkeer:
den morgenstond, de dagen rond
   en de avonden nog meer!

Wanneer alleen ik tranen ween
   't zij droevig 't zij blij,
ik misse u, o ik misse u zoo,
   ik misse u neffens mij!

Zoo mist, voorwaar, zijn wederpaar
   geen veugelken in 't net;
zoo mist geen kind hoe teerbemind,
   zijn moeder noch zij het!

Nu zingt men wel en 't orgelspel
   en misse ik niet, o neen,
maar uwen zang mist de orgelklank
   en misse ik al met een.

Ik misse u als er leugen valsch
   wil monkelen zoo gij loecht,
wanneer gij zacht mij verzen bracht
   of verzen mededroegt.

Ik misse u nog ... waar hoeft u toch,
   waar hoeft u niet gezeid ...
Ach! 'k heb zoo dikwijls heimelijk
   God binnen u geleid!

Daar misse ik u, daar misse ik u
   zoo dikwijls, en, ik ween:

I MISS YOU

to an absent friend

I miss you when I go away,
whenever I return:
at morning and all through the day,
all evening still I burn!

When I alone weep copious tears
of sadness or of glee,
I miss you, oh, I miss you so,
I miss you next to me!

No bird so misses, it is true,
its partner in the net;
no child, however dearly loved,
its mother, nor she it!

Now we sing and organ peals
I do not miss, oh no,
but your voice is missing from the sounds
and that I'm missing so.

I miss you when a false pretence
attempts to sound like you,
when you so softly brought me verse
or took my verse with you.

I miss you still ... where you don't need;
no need to say to you ...
Oh! so often secretly
I've put God into you!

There I miss you, miss you there
so often, and I weep:

geen hope meer op wederkeer,
   geen hope meer, o neen!

Geen hope, neen, geen hoop, hoe kleen,
   die 't leven overschiet';
maar in den schoot der goede dood
   en misse ik u toch niet?

EEN DREUPEL POESIJ

aan Gustaf Verriest

Hoe blij is de arme vogel toen
   hij, lange lang geboeid,
weêrom zijn vlerk mag opendoen
   en in den hemel roeit!
En hoe is 't arme vischken blij,
   dat, in mijn net gepakt,
half dood gesperteld, los van mij
   weêrom in 't water smakt!
het gouden vliegsk' hoe blijde ruischt
   het, werk- en worstelensmoe,
wanneer ik zijn gevange, mijn vuist,
   ontluikend opendoe!
Zoo blij en is mijn ziele niet,
   maar zeven maal zoo blij,
wanneer ik, moet en mat, geniet
   een dreupel poesij.—
In 't vrij bewind des vogels en
   in 't koele ruim daarvan,
en 'k weet niet waar ik nog al ben
   wanneer ik dichten kan:
't gedacht springt als de visch, die zeer
   in 't waterkrystalijn

no hope is left of your return,
no hope for me to keep!

No hope, no hope, however small,
can manage to survive;
but in the lap of kindly death
my longing won't stay alive?

(PV)

A DROP OF POETRY

to Gustaf Verriest

How happy is the poor bird when
He, tied up for so long,
May open up his wings again
And skywards wing in song!
How happy is the baby trout
That, caught up in my net,
Exhausted, dying, now let out,
Plops back into the wet!
How gladly hums the golden fly
Escaping from the gloom,
When I release him by and by
From hands that were his tomb!
My soul knows not such perfect joy,
But is seven times as blest,
When tired and empty I enjoy
A verse within my breast.–
Within the bird's own realm of air
And spaces cool and free,
Myself am lost, I know not where,
When poetry comes to me;
The thought leaps like the fish that shines
In water crystal clear,

blank blinkt en weêrom blinkt, aleer
'k hem wel gewaar kan zijn;
bepereld als het vliegske, licht
en schitterend in de zon,
zoo vliegt en lacht het los gedicht
met zijnen Dichter ton:
neen, blij en is mijn ziel toen niet,
maar is iets meer als blij,
wanneer zij, God zij dank, geniet,
een dreupelken poesij!

GOD IS DAAR

of de zegen met de Alderheiligste

Klinkt en rinkelt de heldere belle,
klinkt de klenkerende autaarschelle,
bonst het ronkende klokgeklop,
reekt het riekende reukvat op
Rukt het rookende reukvat neder,
rukt en rinkel 'et weg en weder,
slaat het wentelend orgel spel,
drukt de dreunende terden fel,
doet de bronzene monden spreken,
dat de daverende ruiten breken,
dat de kerke vol klanken komt,
en van de zwellende zangen dromt.,
buigt uw biddende hoofden neder
klopt en klopt op uw' herten weder,
buigt en bidt en klopt en ziet
naar den grond, in den hemel niet:
buigt, onkundigen, buigt, geleerden,
buigt, vernederden, buigt vereerden:
God is daar! Hij rijst ... Hij daalt,
en Zijn goudene kroone straalt
weg en weder voor die schouwen

And flashes pale so many times
Before I see him near;
Bejewelled like the fly so light
And sparkling in the sun
So flies and laughs the poet's flight
And takes the poet as one;
No, that is not my soul's true cheer,
But is much more of course,
When she, thank God, is granted here,
A modicum of verse.

(PK)

GOD IS THERE

or the Blessed Sacrament

Set the bells in the bell-tower swinging,
set the sanctuary hand-bell ringing,
praises from every brazen throat!
see the clouds of incense float,
See, as the altar-candles blaze,
how the polished censer sways,
Work the bellows with a will,
heave upon the lever till,
hark! the flood of the organ-strains
beats upon walls and window-panes
till all the strength of sound and stone
are made inseparably one.
Bow in prayer to the floor,
beat your breast and beat once more,
bow and bid and beat, and know
that heaven is high and you are low,
Bow down, simple and learned, bow,
great or lowly equal now,
Then, as your humble faces rise,
see God himself before your eyes
raised aloft in gesture wide;

en zijn oogen op durft hou'en,
kruiswijs, ende ... God is daar,
JESUS, God en mensch voorwaar,
God, met lichaam ziel en leven,
God, voor Wien al de engelen beven,
liggende rondom 't altaar:
buigt u, buigt u ... God is daar!

*

Als de ziele luistert
Spreekt het al een taal dat leeft,
't lijzigste gefluister
ook een taak en teeken heeft:
blâren van de boomen
kouten met malkaar gezwind,
baren in de stroomen
klappen luid en welgezind,
winde en wee en wolken,
wegelen van Gods heiligen voet,
talen en vertolken
't diep gedoken Woord zoo zoet ...
als de ziele luistert!

TER INLEIDINGE

Op harpe ende luyt speelt nu elck een
So dede ick oock, maer hebbe er gheen.

Schavende snijdt het staal
En 't kerft in de penne van cederhout:
zacht is het herte des houts,
zacht en sterk is de penne van ceder,

recall Your Saviour crucified,
He is there, both God and Man,
joined in our salvation's plan,
Jesus, Body and Soul entire,
who sets the longing heart on fire,
Your very God is present there;
Bow your head again in prayer.

(AE)

*

When the soul listens,
Everything speaks in a language that lives
Even the slightest whisper
Has a language and meaning:
The leaves on the trees
Converse together in hurried whispers
The wavelets of the stream
Babble clearly and merrily
The sighing winds and clouds,
Though far away from God's Holy Throne
Tell of and interpret
The sweet mystery of His Hidden Word ...
When the soul listens!

(MS)

INTRODUCTION

On harps and lutes they play each one
I'd do so too, but I have none.

Shaving, the steel now cuts
and slices the pen of cedar wood;
soft is the heart of the wood,
soft and strong is the pen of cedar,

zacht als het hout van het kruis,
sterk als het kruise des Heeren.
Zoet riekt het hout als den balsem van Libanon,
zoet als de reukende wasemen Sions,
zoet als de biddende wolke die stijgt in den tempel.
Sterk is het hout en sterk is de penne:
sterk zij de tale der woorden!
Weg met u, penne, over 't gladde papier,
uwe eigene bane en uw land is 't!
Vaart op het gladde papier,
in de hand die u voert,
en die zelfdoor een ziele gevoerd wordt!
Weg met u, penne, vooruit,
't zij de schauw van het wentlende loof
geplekt op het blanke papier valt,
't zij dat de klimmende zon
mijn stappen met schaduw vooruitbeeldt,
't zij ze, mij, penne, en u zelf
van schaduw verlangende, wegzinkt!
Weg met u, penne,
over 't gladde papier,
en rust niet, en rust niet,
tot dat de ziele
het zwellende tij des gevoels,
hare eigene krachten geen meester,
los en heur banden haast kwijt,
in brekende tranen vooruitstrooint!
Ligt dan, nutteloos hout,
en rust, met de hand van den dichter,
rust, dan kunt gij de ziele
een last maar geen hulpe zijn:
rust dan!

soft as the wood of the cross,
strong as the cross of the Saviour.
Sweet the wood smells like the balm of Lebanon,
sweet, as the perfumed mists of Zion,
sweet as the clouds of prayer that rise in the temple,
strong is the wood and strong the pen:
may the language of words be strong too!
Off you go, pen, across the smooth paper,
your very own path and your country!
Career across the smooth paper,
in the hand that bears you
and itself by a soul is carried!
Off you go, pen, go on,
be it that the shadows of tumbling leaves
fall in patches on the blank paper,
be it that the rising sun
prefigures my steps with shadow,
be it that it sinks from me, the pen and yourself,
with lengthening shadows departs!
Off you go, pen,
across the smooth paper,
and rest not, and rest not,
until the soul
the swelling tide of feeling,
no more in control of its strength,
free, almost rid of its bonds,
flows onwards with bursting tears!
Lie then, useless wood,
and rest, with the hand of the poet,
rest, and then you can be
not a burden, but help to the soul:
rest then!

(PV)

KERKHOFBLOMMEN (fragment)

Zoo daar ooit een blomke groeide
over 't graf waarin gij ligt,
of het nog zoo schoone bloeide:
zuiver als liet zonnelicht,
blank gelijk een Lelie blank is,
vonklende als een roozenhert,
needrig als de needre rank is
van de winde daar m' op terdt,
riekend, vol van honing, ende
geren van de bie bezocht,
nog en waar 't, voor die U kende,
geen dat U gelijken mocht!

GIJ BADT OP EENEN BERG

Gij badt op eenen berg alleen,
en ... JESU, ik en vind er geen
waar 'k hoog genoeg kan klimmen
om U alleen te vinden:
de wereld wil mij achterna,
alwaar ik ga
of sta
of ooit mijn oogen sla;
en arm als ik en is er geen,
geen een,
die nood hebbe en niet klagen kan;
die honger, en niet vragen kan;
die pijne, en niet gewagen kan
hoe zeer het doet!
o Leert mij, armen dwaas, hoe dat ik bidden moet!

CHURCHYARD FLOWERS (fragment)

Take any flower that ever grows
over the grave in which you lie,
be it the loveliest flower that blows,
pure as the sunlit summer sky,
white as when the snowdrop peeps,
flushed as the rose's nodding head,
lowly as when bindweed creeps
with tendrils under passing tread,
fragrant with such honey breath
as draws the heavy-burdened bee
yet none there is in life or death
could figure what you were to me.

(AE)

YOU PRAYED ON THE MOUNTAINSIDE, ALONE

You prayed on the mountainside, alone,
but ... Jesu, there's no mountain, none,
high enough where I can climb
and find you there, alone:
the world purges,
wherever I go
or turn
or cast my eye;
and poor as I am there is none,
nor one
who's needy and cannot complain;
hungry, and cannot beg; whom pain
tortures, and he cannot say
how bitterly!
Oh, teach this idiot, teach him how to pray!

(JBr)

BLIJDSCHAP

Ja! Daar zijn blijde dagen nog in 't leven,
   hoe weinig ook, daar zijnder nog voorwaar,
  en geren zou ik alles, alles geven
    om één van die, mijn God, om éénen maar,
  wanneer ik U gevoel, U heb, U drage,
   mij onbewust, U zelf ben, mij niet meer,
  U noemen kan, mijn God, en zonder klagen,
   herhalen: God! mijn God en lieve Heer!
  o Blijft bij mij, Gij Zon van alle klaarheid,
   o blijft bij mij, blaakt deur end deur mij nu,
  o blijft bij mij, één dingen, één is waarheid,
   al 't ander al is leugen buiten U!
Gij zijt mijn troost, toen alle troost venijn is,
   Gij zijt mijn hulpe, als niemand helpt, elk vlucht,
Gij zijt mijn vreugde, als elke vreugde een pijne is,
   'Hallelujah,' als alles weent en zucht ...
Wat gaat mij om in 't wondere van die stonden,
   Als 't hert mij gloeit en de oog mij berst, en ik,
van tranen dronk, onmachtig ril ten gronde
   en in een storm van liefde en vreugde stik!
Ben ik het nog die weene? ...
   Ben ik het nog die in de stem der winden
Uw spreken hoor, mijn JESU, Uwe taal
   in alle taal, hoe kleen ook, wedervinde,
en Uw gedaante in iederen blommenstaai? ...
   ben ik liet nog die duizend levens wou voor
U, mijn God, en iederen mensche laten,
   en, zelfvergeten, lachend sterven zou? ...

JOY

There are still joyful days in life!
How few they be, still there are some of them.
And gladly I would give up all and everything
For one of these, my God for a single one of these:
When I feel Thee, possess Thee, carry Thee,
And, losing my own consciousness, am one with Thee, not any longer myself.
When I call Thee: My god! And far from suffering and pain,
Repeat: God! My God, my dearest Lord!
O remain with me, Thou Sun of all clearness,
O remain with me, pierce me with ardent glow thru and thru.
O remain with me. One single thing, one only is the truth,
– and all is lie but Thou.
Thou art my consolation, when all human consolation is venom,
Thou art my help when no one helps, but flies.
Thou art my joy when all other joy is painful,
the Hallelujah when everything weeps and sighs ...
What happens then to me in the wonder of these moments,
when my heart glows, my eyes burst forth in tears,
till I, drunken with weeping, shudder to unconsciousness on the floor
and disappear in a storm of love and happiness?
Am I the one who weeps?...
Am I the one who in the tongue of the winds
hear Thy whisper, my Jesus? Who listen to Thy voice
in the voice of everything, however small it be,
and perceive Thy own self in each flower?
Am I the one who wishing for a thousand lives
To lose for Thee and for every man on earth,
Who would gladly die, in self-forgetfulness and with a radiant smile of joy?....

(GR)

HOORT 'T IS DE WIND

Hoort, 't is de wind, 't is de wind, 't is de wind, en
   zoekende zucht hij om ruste te vinden,
   overal rond, en en vindt geene, nooit:
   of hij de daken van d'huizen verstrooit,
of hij de vliegende blaren doet ruischen,
of hij de boomen daarboven doet buischen,
   of hij de torren hun toppen afwaait,
   of hij de malende meulenen draait,
of hij de zee in de wolken doet botsen,
of hij ze slaat op heur zuchtende rotsen,
   of hij de schepen daarbinnen begraaft,
   of hij door 't schuimbekkend zeewater draaft:
nimmer en vindt hij, de wind, 't is de wind, en
nimmer en zal hij geen ruste meer vinden,
   nimmer en rustt' hij maar eenen keer: 'Stil!'
   sprak Hij, die immer in ruste is 'Ik wil!'
   sprak Hij die nog alles in roer zetten kan:
   'Stil!' en hij rustte ... en hij rustte nochtan!

            *

'k Hoore tuitend' hoornen en
   de navond is nabij
      voor mij:
kinderen, blij en blonde, komt,
   de na vond is nabij,
      komt bij:
zegene u de Alderhoogste, want
   de navond is nabij
      komt bij:
'k hoore tuitend'hoornen en
   de navond is nabij,
      voor mij!

HARK! IT'S THE WIND

Hark it's the wind, it's the wind, it's the wind!
Seeking, it sighs, but no rest can it find.
Everywhere round, it seeks peace and finds none,
Whether it tumbles the roofing-tiles down,
Whether it whirls through the rustling leaves.
Until the vast forest tosses and heaves,
or whether it roars round the spire and the vane,
or flaps the mill sails as they rip under strain
or tangles its hands in the sea's hoary locks,
or dashes in foam on the lurking rocks,
or plunges the ship neath the whelming waves
and over the pitiless surface raves,
it never finds rest. It's the wind, it's the wind!
Nevermore rest shall its blast ever find,
Nevermore rest till once ordered, 'Still!'
by One who is peace and omnipotent will.
He speaks, who is master and maker of peace:
'Still!' and it rests, and its howlings cease.

(AE)

*

Hark, bugles are calling and
the nightfall darkens
nearer:
Children, come now blonde and blithe,
as nightfall darkens,
near me:
Scaled with the Father's sign you are, for
the nightfall darkens,
hear me:
Hark, bugles are calling
and the night falls darkening
nearer.

(YL)

BOERKE NAAS

Wie heeft er ooit het lied gehoord,
    het lied van Boerke Naas?
't En ha', 't is waar, geen leeuwenhert,
    maar toch, hij was niet dwaas.

Boer Naas die was twee runders
    gaan verkoopen naar de steê
en bracht, als hij naar huis toe kwam,
    zes honderd franken meê.

Boer Naas, die maar een boer en was,
    nochtans was scherp van zin,
hij ging en kocht een zevenschot,
    en stak daar kogels in.

Alzoo kwam Naas, met stapkes licht,
    en met de beurze zwaar;
hij zei: 'Och 'k wilde dat ik thuis
    en in mijn bedde waar!'

Al met nen keer, wat hoort boer Naas,
    juist bacht hem in den tronk?
Daar roert entwat, daar loert entwat:
    't docht Naasken dat 't verzonk!

En, eer dat 't ventjen asem kreeg,
    zoodanig was 't ontsteld,
daar grijpen Naas twee vuisten vast,
    en 't ligt daar, neêrgeveld.

't En hoorde noch 't en zag bijkan,
    't en voelde bijkans niet,
't en zij dat 't een pistole zag,
    en, zeggen hoorde: ' ... Ik schiet!'

FARMER NICK

Come lads and lasses, gather round,
and I'll ye of Farmer Nick –
although no lionheart was he,
by gum, he was hard to trick!

One day our Nick he took to town
two cows, to see them sold,
and by the eve his purse was full
with twenty coins of gold.

Our Nick was a simple farming man,
but gormless he was not,
a seven-shooter he did buy
with seven leaden shot.

He started home with heavy purse,
and lightly he did tread,
'By 'eck, I wish,' our Nick did say,
'I were back 'ome i' bed.'

While passing by a hollow tree,
he hears a sudden sound –
did something lurk, did something move,
and drop down to the ground?

But ere our Nick can breathe a breath,
it's up with him, alas –
he's grabbed by a pair of beefy fists
and knocked flat on the grass.

The blow it blinds our Farmer Nick,
his head and ears are numb,
and then he sees a pistol black
and hears, 'I'll shoot, by gum

'Ik schiet, zoo gij, op staanden voet,
   niet al uw geld en geeft;
en g' hebt, van zoo gij roert, me man,
   uw laatsten dag geleefd!'

Boer Naas, die alle dagen vijf
   zes kruisgebeden bad,
om lang te mogen leven, peist
   hoe hij in nesten zat!

'Wat zal ze zeggen,' kreesch boer Naas,
   'wanneer ik t'huiswaard keer?
Hij heeft het weêrom al verhuisd!
   die zatlap, nog nen keer!'

'Hoort hier, mijn vriend, believe 't u,
   toogt dat gij minzaam zijt,
och, schiet ne kogel deur mijn hoed
   en spaart mij 't vrouwverwijt!

'k Zal zeggen, als ik thuis geraak:
   men heeft mijn geld geroofd,
en, lutter schilde 't, of ik had
   nen kogel deur mijn hoofd!'

De dief, die meer van kluiten hield
   als van boer Naas zijn bloed,
schoot rap ne kogel deur end deur
   de kobbe van z'nen hoed.

'Bedankt!' zei Naas, en greep zijn slep:
   'schiet nog een deur mijn kleed!'
De dief legt aan en Naasken houdt
   zijn pitelerken g'reed.

'Schiet nog een deur mijn broek,' zei Naas,
   'toen peist me wijf, voorwaar,

I'll shoot thee dead, if tha don't give
yon purse that's full o' gold,
an' if tha moves or lifts a limb,
thy funeral bell 'as tolled!'

Our Nick, who once or twice a week
says catechisms six
so God might spare him till he's old,
now thinks, 'Boy,' 'ere's a fix!'

'Aye,' says Nick, 'but wait on, lad –
it's what our lass will think,
she'll say, "I know thee, drunken sot,
tha's spent it all o' drink!"

A victim of a woman's wrath
I fear that I might fall,
show kindness, lad, and through my 'at,
pray shoot a pistol ball!

And then I'll say, when I gets 'ome,
"Tha's lucky I'm not dead:
my money robbed, and a pistol ball
all but through my 'ead!"'

The robber he was fond of gold,
and Nick of life and limb,
so the robber took the farmer's hat
and shot it through the brim.

'Why, ta,' says Nick, 'but an 'ole through my coat
would surely save me shame!'
And he held the tails of his old gaberdine
while the robber took his aim.

'An' shoot one,' Nick said, 'through my kecks
and then, by gum, the wife

als dat ik, bij mirakel, ben
    ontsnapt aan 't lijfsgevaar.'

De roover zegt: 'Nu zal 't wel gaan,
    waar is uw beurze, snel:
'k en heb noch tijd noch kogels meer ...'
    'Ik wel,' zegt Naas, 'ik wel!'

Zijn zevenschot haalt Naas toen uit
    en spreekt: 'Is 't dat ge u niet,
in een-twee-drie, van hier en pakt,
    gij galgendweil, ik schiet!

'Ik schiet, van als gij nader komt,
    uw dommen kop in gruis,
en, zoo gij Naas nog rooven wilt,
    laat uw verstand niet thuis!'

En loopen dat die roover dei,
    de beenen van zijn lijf,
zoo snel dat 't onbeschrijflijk is,
    hoe snel ook dat ik schrijf!

Hier stoppe ik. Dichte een ander nu
    ne voois op boerke Naas;
't is waar, 't en was geen leeuwenhert,
    maar toch. 't en was niet dwaas!

*

Slaapt, slaapt, kindtje slaapt,
    en doet uwe oogskes toe,
die pinkelende winkelende oogskes daar,
    'k ben 't wiegen al zoo moe:
'k en kan u niet meer wiegen,

she'll think it's by a miracle,
that I've come back wi' my life!'

The robber says, 'Nay lad, it's time
to 'and thy purse to me,
for I've got no more pistol shot–'
' 'Ere's shot' cries Nick, 'for thee!'

His seven-shooter Nick pulls out
and holds to the robber's head,
and then Nick says, 'Be off, mak' sharp,
or I'll fill thee full o' lead!

Aye, gallow-rag, come show thy 'eels,
or I'll blast thy brains to foam,
an' next time tha'd rob Farmer Nick
don't leave thy sense at 'ome!'

Up sprang the robber, one two three,
and scampered off pell-mell
he ran so fast that where he went
not even I can tell!

And now I've told ye all I know
about good Farmer Nick,
Although no lionheart was he,
by gum, he was hard to trick!

(FJ)

*

Sleep, baby, sleep!
Close your eyelids, do!
Close your wandering, wondering eyes,
For I am tired too.
I can no longer rock you,

'k en ga u niet meer wiegen,
slaapt, slaapt, toe!
g'Hebt uw hert- en uw mondtje voldaan,
g'hebt al uw krinkelde krullejes aan,
ach en'k en kan van uw wiegske niet gaan:
slaapt, slaapt, toe!

1860

GELUKKIG KIND

Gelukkig kind,
dat ligt en laat geworden
al't geen den mensch
zoo driftiglijk beroert!

Gelukkig kind,
dat niet en peist op morgen,
dat alles mint,
en nijdig niets beloert!

Gelukkig kind,
dat elken stap in 't leven
een stap vernaarst
aan 't heilig kinderland!

Gelukkig kind,
'k zou alles alles geven
voor uw geluk, mijn kind, 'dat ligt en roert in't zand!

I will no longer rock you.
Sleep then, do!
Sweet, heart, sweet mouth, sweet curly head,
I cannot go from your baby bed
I'll stay beside it then instead,
Sleep, baby, sleep!

(AE)

1860

HAPPY CHILD

O happy child,
That lies and lets develop
All that moves mankind
So frantically withal!

O happy child,
That cares not for the morrow
Loves all so mild,
And covets nought at all!

O happy child,
Moving through life alone
Approaches step by step
The blessed children's land.

O happy child!
I'd give all, all I own
For your happiness, my child, lying digging in the sand!

(PK)

'S AVONDS

't Wordt al sterre dat men ziet
in dat hoog en blauw verschiet daar,
blijde sterren, anders niet,
in dat hoog en blauw verschiet.

't Wordt hier altijd al verdriet,
van dat oud en zwart verdriet daar,
't wordt hier altijd anders niet
als dat oud en zwart verdriet.

Laat mij, laat mij, in 't verdriet,
vliegen naar dat hoog verschiet daar,
waar men al die sterren ziet,
al die sterren, ... anders niet!

*

Daar liep een dichtje in mijn gebed,
en 'k wilde 't aan den kant gezet,
maar, niet te doen, het wilde, en 't zou
mij plagen, als ik bidden wou!
En *nu is* mijn gebed gedaan,
en 't dichtje is 'k weet niet waar gegaan:
vergeefs gezocht, vergeefs, o wee,
'k en vinde rijm noch dichtje meer!

*

Gij zegt dat 't Vlaamsch te niet zal gaan:
't en zal!
Dat 't waalsch gezwets zal boven slaan:
't en zal!
Dat hopen, dit begeren wij:

EVENING

Only stars shine far and wide
in that lofty blue outspread,
happy stars, and nought beside
in that lofty blue outspread,

here is nothing else but grief
in our age-old world of pain,
here no promise of relief
from our age-old world of pain,

let me in my sorrow be
lifted to that heaven there
where are only stars to see;
lift me to that heaven there.

(AE)

*

A little verse ran through my prayer
I tried to banish it right there
And then, but not a hope, 't will stay
To haunt me when I want to pray ...
And now I've finished with my prayer
The verse is gone I know not where!
In vain the search, in vain alack!
The rhyme or poem will not come back.

(PK)

*

You say that Flemish soon will die:
Not so!
That dull Walloon will it outvie:
Not so!
This is our hope, our fervent prayer:

dat zeggen en dat zweren wij:
zoo lange als wij ons weren, wij:
't en zal,'t en zal,
't en zal!

TOT DE ZONNE

Zonne, als 'k in mijn groene blaren
en vol waterpeerlen sta
en dat gij komt uitgevaren,
schouwt mijn bloeiend herte u na.
Throonend op den throon gezeten
van den rooden dageraad,
wilt het blomke niet vergeten,
dat naar u te wachten staat.

Langs die hooge hemelpaden,
zonne, nimmer klemmens moe,
volge ik u, van zoo 'k mijn bladen
met den morgen opendoe;
komt en zoekt mijn herte en vindt het,
u behoort het, u bemint het,
u verwacht het, u bemint het,
die mijn hemelminnaar zijt.

's Avonds, als het wordt te donkeren,
als ge in 't gloeiend westen daalt,
schouw ik naar uw laatste vonkelen
zinken met u nederwaard.
Hangende op mijn staal gebogen,
weene ik toen den nacht rondom,
van u niet te aanschouwen mogen:
kom toch weêre, o zonne, kom!

*

This is our claim, 't is this we swear
While we have Flemish breath to spare:
Not so, Not so,
Not so!

(JI)

TO THE SUN

O Sun, when I stand in my green leaves,
With my petals full of dew,
And you fare forth in your splendour,
My blossoming heart looks to you.
When, on the red dawn throning,
The world at your feet you view,
Forget not the little flower
That waits and watches for you!

O Sun, You that climb never tired
The lofty paths of the skies,
My leaves, that open to see you,
Follow you as you rise ...
Come and seek out my heart and find it,
For you it lives and dies!
It waits for you, it loves you ...
O my Bridegroom from Paradise!

And when in the evening the dark comes,
When you haste to the welcoming West,
O watch Your last beams fading,
I see you sink down to rest.
With my head bowed I weep till the morning,
Forsaken and distressed.
Come back, my Beloved, I am waiting
To rise up and be caressed!
(JBi)

*

Hoe stille is 't als de donder dreegt,
en, al met eens, ontschakeld,–
gelijk Gods hofhond, belt en bast
en door de wolken rakelt!
Het water speit en 't vier dooreen,
geruchtte is 't en gerommel
dat bomt en bamt en wederbelt,
gelijk nen wolkentrommel.

Het hagelt en de wind ontbindt
zijne alderfelste vlagen,
en 't is alsof hij kegelspeelde,
met tien duist donderslagen!

NIET
Daar wandelde op nen Zomerdag,
een neuswijze achter 't land,
daar hij twee kleene meiskes zag
die speelden in het zand.

Zei neuswijs: 'Maar, wat doet gij daar,
gij meiskes allebei?
Wat doet ge daar gij blond van haar,
gij meiskes, in de Mei?

En 't eene van de meiskes zei:
   'Wel heere, zoo ge ziet
wij zitten hier, wij zitten, hei!
   wij zitten, en 'n doen niet.'

'Maar niet,' zoo zei de neuswijs mij,
   'dat is een ding, gewis
dat is een dingen dat ge gij
   niet weet wat dat het is.'

How still before the thunder comes
until it bursts its shackles
and like a watchdog bay and growls
all yellow teeth and hackles!
The through the rain and lightning flash
we feel the tumult coming;
it booms and bangs and echoes round
and sets the cloud-rack drumming.
Down comes the hail as wind with wrath
Gives voice to fiercest squalling.
Thus might be in a bowling-alley
a thousand skittles falling.

(AE)

NOTHING

A cocky man one summer day
was roaming through the land,
and there he found two maids at play,
at play upon the sand,

Said he, 'What are you doing there,
you pretty maidens twain?
tell me now, you blond of hair,
you maidens, tell me plain.'

And thus he heard one of them say:
'Well, surely it is clear,
we're sitting down, we're sitting, eh?
and doing nothing here.'

'But nothing!' said the cocky one,
'now that's a thing, I fear,
a thing, when all is said and done,
which you don't know, my dear!'

'Ik doe,' zei 't ouder meiske boos,
   - en 't wiste entwat dervan–
'niet Is een kouse voeteloos,
   en zonder been deran.'

*

1861

't Zij vroeg of laat
daar niets en baat,
daar moet elk tol betalen:
't zij munk of non, gij, nu, ik ton:
de dood komt alles halen!

1862

'T LAATSTE

aan den onbekenden lezer

Hoe zoet is 't om te peizen dat,
   terwijl ik rust misschien,
een ander, ver van hier, mij on-
   bekend en nooit gezien,
u lezen kan, mijn dichten, mijn
   geliefde, en niet en weet
van al de droeve falen van
   uw vader den Poëet!
Hoe blij en is't gedacht niet, als
   ik neêrzitte ende peis,
u volgend waar gij loopt op uw
   gezwinde wereldreis,
dat, zondig en ellendig als
   ik ben, geliefde kroost,

'I do!' the older maiden said,
a sock without a foot!' –
Then waggishly she tossed her head;
'nor yet a leg to boot!'

(AE)

*

1861

Right soon or late
comes ruthless fate
and everyone must pay;
or monk, or nun, we, everyone,
by death are borne away.

(AE)

1862

THE LAST

to the unknown reader

How sweet indeed it is to think,
while I'm at rest maybe,
another, far from here, unknown
and never seen by me,
can read you then, my poetry,
beloved, and is unaware
Of all the inadequacies of
the poet who sired you there!
How happy is the thought, when I
sit down and contemplate,
and follow, where you lead,
your world trip's lightning rate,
that, sinful and wretched as
I am, my offspring dear,

uw stem, waarin geen zonde 'n zit,
	misschien een ander troost;
uw stemme kan verblijden, schoon
	hij droef zij die u miek:
uw stemme kan genezen, zij
	uw Dichter nog zoo ziek:
uw stem misschien doet bidden, wijl
	ik zuchte en, biddensmoê,
versteend zitte en mijn herte noch
	mijne oogen opendoe!
o Dichten, die 'k gedregen, die 'k
	gebaard hebbe, in de pijn
des dichtens, en gevoedsterd aan
	dit arem herte mijn;
mijn dichten, die'k zoo dikwijls her-
	castijd heb, hergekleed,
bedauwend met mijn tranen en
	besproeiend met mijn zweet,
o spreekt voor mij, mijn dichten, als
	God eens mij reden vraagt,
is 't zake dat gij, krankgeboor-
	nen, 't arme leven draagt
tot verder als mijn grafstede, en
	niet sterft aleer ik sterf:
o 'n weze 't dan om u niet dat
	ik daar het Leven derf!

your voice, in which there is no sin,
may offer someone cheer;
Your voice can give delight, although
he who made you may be sad;
your voice can heal, though it may be
that his affliction's bad;
your voice can make men pray, while
I sigh and, tired of prayer,
sit just like stone, don't open heart
or eyes to see what's there!
O verses that in me I've borne
and given birth, felt labour's pain
for poetry, and nourished
from this poor heart again;
my verses, which so many times
I've reclothed and reset,
watered with my bitter tears
and sprinkled with my sweat,
oh speak for me, my verses, if
God one day asks wherefore,
it's vital that you, born
in sickness, carry my life before,
beyond where lies my tombstone,
don't die before I'm dead:
let it not be on your account
that I lay down my head!

(PV)

HANGT NEN TRUISCH

Hangt nen truisch hem over 't hoofd,
    van de leeuwerk,
    van de leeuwerk,
hangt nen truisch hem over 't hoofd,
eer gij hem de vrijheid rooft.

Als hij rijst, de kevie moe,
    dan vliegt hij,
    dan vliegt hij,
als hij rijst, de kevie moe,
niet zijn hoofd en hert ten bloe'.

Ah, de vrijheid is zoo zoet ...
    gouden kevie,
    gouden kerker:
ah, de vrijheid is zoo zoet ...
liever vrij – als alle goed!

1866

HEIDENSCH LIED

Nu, zwijgt van Troyen en voortaan
    Van Œacus gezwegen!
Wat gaat ons al die rijmram aan
Van voorvaars driemaal negen?
Laat Inachus en Codrus daar:
Ze rusten in het graf voorwaar,
    En, eer dat wij daarbij zijn,
Zoo ga de tasse omhooge maar
    En laat ons nog eens blij zijn!

HANG A SASH

Hang a sash above the crown,
of the skylark,
of the skylark,
hang a sash above its crown,
before you catch and tie it down.

When it climbs, tired of the cage,
it will not fly,
it will not fly,
when it climbs, tired of the cage,
and cut its head and heart in rage.

Oh, one's freedom is so sweet ...
golden cages,
golden prisons:
oh, one's freedom is so sweet ...
better free – than gold replete!

(PV)

1866

PAGAN SONG

Make no lament for Troy,
for Oeacus no moan;
seek neither pain nor joy
in generations gone;
leave Inachus and Codrus where
their ash lies covered up,
before we living join them there
make wassail, fill the cup!

De wijn, de wijn
   Hij mag er zijn:
De beste bezen boven,
Die groeien aan de takken fijn
Van Chios blijde hoven!
    Hoepsa!
  Naar de amphora:
Hoeverre is ze al geschoven?

*

1870

't Is uit nu met droefheid en smerte en getraan;
    't uit nu met Heer Jesus zijn lijden!
De Kerke trekt weder haar feestgewaad aan,
    zoo, juichende, zingt ij den blijden
        Halleluja!

Triomph! Roept de booze, en hij meent dat de Kerk
    verzwakt is, en valt in den strijd, en
hij waakt bij haar graf! Maar zij wentelt den zerk
    van 't hoofd, en zij zingt weêr den blijden
        Halleluja!

Lijk Kerke en lijk Christus, met haar en met hem
    is 't zoete te strijden, te lijden!
voor ons is de zege, en met juichende stem
    zoo zingen wij zalig den blijden
        Halleluja!

*

O fill with wine
your cup and mine,
O fill again and fill,
from grapes that grow,
row on row
on every Chios hill.
Hurrah! Hurrah!
the amphora
will cure us all of ill.

(AE)

*

1870

It's all over with sorrow and tears;
it's over with Jesus's pain.
The church is clothed in her festival garb,
and joyfully sings her refrain:
Hallelujah!

Triumph! So Satan declares, and he thinks that the church
is weakened and falls in the strife,
and he lurks by her tomb. But she thrusts her way out
and once more is risen to life:
Hallelujah!

To the church and to Jesus, for her and for Him,
the struggle is sweet, and the pain
For us the battle is won, and rejoicing we sing,
as Our Saviour rises again:
Hallelujah!

(AE)

*

1872

Verloren moeite, onnuttig streven,
Om langer als den tijd te leven
   Dien God in zijn beschik, ons stelt:
   Zijt keizer, koning, oorlogsheld,
Zijt jong of oud, zijt rijk aan gaven
Of arm, gij sterft, gij wordt begraven ...
   't Is al voorbij, verleên, gedaan!
   Toch neen, daar blijft iets voortbestaan,
Dat meest veracht wordt en misprezen,
Dat is, en dat zal eeuwig wezen ...
   Past op uw ziele, o mensch, en doet
   Hetgeen God wil, hetgeen gij moet.
Laat lachen al die lachen konnen:
De ziel gered is 't all gewonnen;
   En die dit één verliezen zal
   Verliest, eilaas, het al!

1877

O DICHTERGEEST

   O Dichtergeest van al wat banden
   hebt gij mij, armen knecht, verlost,
     en, uit uw' handen,
wat heeft uw dierste gunst mijn weinig werks gekost!

   Gij Godlijk wezen doet mij leven
   waar menig andre sterven zou,
     en ongegeven
is nog de grootegift waarom 'k u derven wou.

   Gij zijt genezing, en de wonden,
   de diepe, o wondre, toen gij, teer,

1872

Wasted effort, useless strife
to stretch beyond its term the life
which God in his own wisdom gave!
Be emperor, king, or soldier brave,
be rich in talents, young or old,
be poor! You die, your tale is told.
All slips away, is past and gone,
and yet there still is one truth, one,
which, having eyes, men do not see,
which now and evermore shall be.
Beware your soul, o man, and do
whatever God may will for you.
Let all those laugh who so may choose,
but they have everything to lose
while he who keeps his soul unstained
will find himself a whole world gained.

(AE)

1877

O POETRY

O poetry, from many bonds
you have freed me, your poor slave,
and from your hands,
what little effort your favour gave!

You, heavenly being, make me live
where many others would soon die,
and they've yet to give
the great gift for which I'd pass you by.

You are healing wounds I've got
deep down, you marvel; you tenderly

        die hebt gevonden,
getint en toegetast, zijn gave en zonder zeer.

        Hoe menig werf, hoe duizend malen
          Hebt gij, o Geest, mij dit gezeid:
            maar hoe verhalen?
't Gevoel, en zuchte, eilaas, naar uw' welsprekendheid!

EN DURFT GIJ MIJ

En durft gij mij van dichten spreken,
    die nimmer zijt in staat
        twee reken
te rijmen dat het gaat!

Het dichten is van God gegeven,
    maar niet aan elk ende een
        in 't leven;
de kunste is niet gemeen.

Laat bloeien al die roos mag wezen,
    spruit helder, zijt gij bron,
        maar dezen
die ton zijn blijven ton!

De miere en zal geen peerd heur wenschen,
    de krieke geen radijs;
        de menschen
alleen zijn niet zoo wijs.

Zoo, elk ende een liet zijn! Soldaten
    het buskruid, zoo 't behoort,
        gelaten,
en Dichteren het woord!

have found the spot,
sounded and sealed, freed of agony.

How many times, times numberless
have you, o spirit, said to me:
'How to express ...?'
I feel it and sigh, alas, for your fluency!

(PV)

AND DO YOU DARE

And do you dare to speak to me
of poetry, who cannot make
abc
rhyme, for goodness' sake!

Poetry's a gift God gives,
but not to every me
who lives;
art is not currency.

Blossom, all, if you're a rose,
spout clear if you're a spring;
but still those
who're tubs won't sing!

The ant won't wish to be a horse,
the cricket a courgette;
men, of course,
their common sense forget.

So each his own! Those who fight
need powder, as is fit
to ignite,
by poets words are lit!

(PV)

1879

De vlaamsche taal is wonder zoet,
voor wie heur geen geweld en doet,
maar rusten laat in 't herte, alwaar,
ze onmondig leefde en sliep te gaar,
tot dat ze, eens wakker, vrij en vrank,
te monde uitgaat heur vrijen gang!
Wat verruwprachtig hoortooneel,
wat zielverrukkend zingestreel,
o vlaamsche tale, uw' kunste ontplooit,
wanneer zij 't al vol leven strooit
en vol onzegbaar schoonzijn, dat,
lijk wolken wierooks, welt
uit uw zoet wierookvat!

*

1880

o Vrienden, jeunt me een goed gebed,
en peist, eer ge uw betrouwen zet
op al dat ijdle menschen raân,
hoe dat is met mij vergaan!

Ach! jong zijn, dat en heeft, eilaas,
den duur niet van een enklen blaas;
gezond zijn is schier nog zoo broos
als 't ijs waar 't eenen nacht op vroos!

Het leven is één stap, gesteld,
het wiegsken uit, in 't gravenveld!
En dan! o Dan, 'k en weet het niet!
Hij weet 't alleen, die alles ziet!

1879

Our Flemish speech is passing fair,
Yet do not force it from its lair,
The heart within, but let it still
And soundless live and sleep, until
It stir and, with unshackled force,
Pass through the lips upon its course.
Its aural pageant will caress
The senses and the soul no less.
Our speech unfolds that art of sound
While quickening everything around
With beauty, that must nameless be,
Welling like frankincense,
From its sensory.

(AB)

*

1880

O friends, be kind to me and spare
For my poor soul a saving prayer,
Heed not what idle men may say.
Think how my life is sped away.

Our youth is quickly gone, alas!
It is soon shrivelled up like grass,
And health is all too quickly lost
Like rime from one brief night of frost.

Our life is but a step – no more!
From cradle to death's muffled door.
Soon I shall die, I know not when;
He knows alone, who made all men.

Hij weet 't alleen, 't zij heil of ramp,
voor eeuwig, na den wereldkamp,
wat dat er ons te wachten staat,
wanneer de tijd van sterven slaat.

O Dan, mijn God, bermhertigheid,
gij hebt liet aan uw Kruis gezeid:
vergeeft mij wat gj weet en ziet,
want, wat ik deed en wist ik niet!

*

1882

>Alre creature sake ende yerstigheit
>*Ruusbrouck, Bruloft*, p. 108

o Wilde en overvalschte pracht
der blommen, langs den watergracht!

Hoe geren zie 'k u, aangedaan
zoo 't God geliefde, in 't water staan!

Geboren, arg- en schuldeloos,
daar God u eens te willen koos,

daar staat ge: en, in den zonneschijn,
al dat gij doet is blomme zijn!

't Is wezen, 't geen mijn oog aanziet,
't is waarheid gij en dobbelt niet;

en die door u mijn hert verblijdt
is enkel, zoo gij enkel zijt!

Hoe stille is 't En verwaait med al
geen bladtje, dat ons stooren zal:

Once we leave this world of strife
To enter on the after-life,
He knows what we there shall find,
When we shall be no longer blind.

O then, my God, be kind to me,
You promised it upon the tree:
'Forgive these wretches, Father, too,
because they know not what they do.'

(AE)

*

1882

> The essence and prime source of all creatures.
> *Ruusbroec, Bruloft*, p. 108

O wild and perfect harmony
of flowers along the water-way!

How glad I am to see you there
stand in garb God bid you wear!

Born to simple purity,
you stand where God willed you to be,

and there perform through sunlit hours
your simple task – just being flowers!

Pure being thus I see in you
and all you say to me is true;

and the joy which thrills through me
is one with your simplicity.

No leaf astir, so still the air,
peace and silence everywhere

geen rimpelken in 't lief gelaat
des waters, dat vol blommen staat;

geen wind, geen woord: rondom gespreid,
al schaduwe, al stilzwijgendheid!

Dan, diepe, diepe in't water, blauwt,
half groen geblest, de hemelvaut:

en, priemend' hier en daar vergaat
een langgesponnen zonnedraad.

Hoe eerbaar, edel, schoone en fijn
kan toch eene enkele blomme zijn,

die, al med eens, en zorgloos, uit
de hand van heuren Schepper spruit!

Door Hem, en door geen menschenhand,
lag hier een nederig zaad geplant;

door Hem, op dezen oogenblik,
ontlook het, en dien troost heb ik,

dat, blonnne, gij mij bidden doet,
en wezen zoo ik wezen moet:

aanschouwende en bevroedende in
elk uiterste einde 't oorbegin,

den grond van alles; meer gezeid,
maar nog niet al: Gods eerstigheid!

*

No ripple on the water face,
pellucid mirror of your grace!

No wind, no word, but far and wide
shade and peace on every side!

And, flecked with green, another sky
as deep below as heaven is high,

and over all the vista plays
a fan of sunny summer rays.

How holy, noble, lovely, fine
to see a simple flower shine,

so perfectly, so subtly planned
and fashioned by your Maker's hand

By Him, and not by man decreed,
first was sown a humble seed;

and now a flower complete I see,
and this same vision strengthens me;

You signal me a message true
and show what I myself must do,

remembering with simple trust
that, deep in all things, ever must

be hid the universal ground
the everlasting God unbound!

(AE)

*

Wat hangt gij daar te praten
aan die blomme, o bruine bie;
   waarop, waaruit, waarover
ik u ronken hoore en zie?
   Gij zijt er met uw' neuze
met uw' tonge en al ingegaan;
   gij hebt eraan geroken
en van alles aan gedaan,
   daarom, daarin, daarover,
op uw' vlerken alle twee:
   ik wonder hoe die blomme u
Laat geworden, zoo ter lee!
   Och, ware ik in heur' plaatse,
ik het u varen, en ik sloot
   zo seffens al dat werk, al
dat geruchte uit mijnen schoot,
   en 'k ... : 'Rap, uit mijnen weg en
uit mijn zunne, dat ik zie:
   houdt op, en laat mij werken,
of ik strale u!' zei de bie.

               *

1883

   Mijn hert is als een blomgewas,
Dat, opengaande of toegeloken,
   De stralen van de zo zonne vangt,
Of kwijnt en pijnt en hangt gebroken!

   Mijn hert gelijkt het jeugdig groen,
Dat asemt in de daue des morgens;
   Maar zwakt, des avonds, moe geleefd,
Vol stof, vol weemoeds en vol zorgens!

What is it then attracts thee
To the flower, o small brown bee,
Upon which I see thee settling,
Whilst buzzing contentedly?
First thou sendest feelers in,
Then thy tongue to thieve,
For thou hast scented honey,
Which thou pilferest without leave.
Then away on thy wings thou fliest,
When thou hast sipped thy fill:
I wonder why the flower
So willing is, and still.
If I were in its place
I would tell thee to depart,
And banish all that noise
From the centre of my heart.
And I ... 'Quick, out of my way
And light, so that I can see;
Cease chattering, let me work,
Or I'll sting you!' says the bee.

(MS)

*

1883

My heart is like a tender flower,
That, whether in bud or bloom,
Rejoices in the sunshine hour,
Then droops on its broken stem.

My heart is like the fresh young grass
Breathing in the morning dew:
Then, with the approach of even, alas,
Withers in dust and gloom.

    Mijn hert is als een vracht, die wast
En rijp wordt, in de schaduw veholen,
      Aleer de hand des najaar heeft,
Te vroeg eilaas, den boom bestolen!

    Mijn hert gelijkt gelijkt de sterre, die
Vershiet, en aan de hooge wanden
      Des hemels eene sparke strijkt,
Die, eer 'k heraêm, houdt op van branden!

    Mijn herte slacht de regenboog,
Die, hoog gebouwd, dóór al de hemelen,
      Welhaast gedaan heeft rood en blauw
En groen en geluwe en peersch te schemelen!

    Mijn hert ... mijn hertee is krank, en broos,
En onstandvastig in 't verblijden;
      Maar, als 't hem wel gaat éénen stond,
't dagen lang weêr honger lijden!

1886

DRIE DINGEN

Drie dingen bezwaren mijn gemoed:
't eerste is dat ik sterven moet;
't tweede bezwaart mij nog meer;
't is dat ik niet en wete wanneer;
't derde bezwaart mij bovenal:
't dat ik niet en wete
waar ik varen zal!

        *

My heart is like a mellow fruit
Growing, ripening in the sun:
Then Autumn comes, strikes at the root
Of the tree, which dies too soon.

My heart is like a shooting star
Flashing across the heavens high,
And swiftly passing out of sight
Ere I can breathe a sigh.

My heart is like the rainbow bright,
That, spanned across the skies,
Soon loses its prismatic hues,
And fades from mortal eyes.

My heart, my heart is sick and frail,
And fain would have some gladness,
Yet, for one moment's ecstasy,
Can suffer days of sadness.

(MS)

1886

THREE BURDENS

Three burdens weigh upon my heart;
The first that men to death depart.
The second weighs still more on me:
I know not when my death shall be.
The third dismays me most of all;
't is that I know not what
thereafter shall befall!

(AE)

*

1888

De nachtegalen klinken,
    En 't licht doet overal
De bladerholten blinken,
    Tienduizend in 't getal.

De verschgekruinde boomen,
    Ze staan al in de Mei,
Te dampen en te droomen,
    Zoo geurig en zoo vei,

O Zoele Mei, waaromme
    En lijdt gij maar zo lang?
Hoe blijft uw blad, uw blomme
    Zo korten tijd in zwang?

Zoo gij, zo is ons leven,
    Hoe lange het van duur,
Het staat alzoo geschreven,
    Een maand, een dage, een uur.

Een uurke, en zonder zorgen,
    Ach, ware 't mij, o God,
Gelijk den Meidagmorgen,
    Vol zuiver zielgenot!

Doch neen, daar valt te vechten,
    Geen vrede, geen, geen verbei,
Tot dat het, wapenknechten,
    Eens eeuwig worde Mei!

        *

1888

The nightingales are calling,
And over all the sun
Is on the green things falling,
The million and the one.

The trees their steaming tresses
Dry dew-wet in the May,
All in the sun's caresses,
So wanton and so gay.

Oh, May, your lovely bosom
How short a time you bare!
Why is your blade, your blossom,
For such a short time there?

But we, we too, are smitten
When scarce we know our power
Of us no less 'tis written,
A month, a day, an hour.

One short hour without sorrow,
Ah, God! to have it whole,
And like a Mayday morrow,
So clear, so fresh of soul!

But no; for us is shapen
No respite for the fray,
Till each man sheathe his weapon,
And know enduring May.

(KH)

*

1890

o Blomme, die aan niets en hangt,
    of niets bijkans, te blinken;
hoe geren zie 'k uw' lieven tak
    tot mij, als ware 't, zinken!

o Zoete, zoete blommen, laat
    uit ieder van uw' kelken
een dropken mij genieten en
    dan moget gij verwelken.

o Blomme, zoete blomme, kort
    is 't leven van ons beiden:
ge'n bloeit nog maar, g'en blinkt nog maar,
    eene ure, en ... 't al scheiden.

1891

MOEDERKEN

't En is van u hiernederwaard
geschilderd of
    geschreven,
mijn moederken,
geen beeltenis,
geen beeld van u
    gebleven.

Geen teekening
geen lichtdrukmaal
geen beitelwerk
    van steene,
't en zij dat beeld
in mij, dat gij
gelaten hebt,
    alleene.

1890

O flower upon nothing hung,
at most a slender thread,
how prettily it seems as if
to me you nod your head!

O lovely flowerlets, bestow
from every tiny cup
one droplet each for my delight
before we shrivel up!

O blossom, tender blossom, short
the lives of you and me;
we flourish here upon the earth
one hour – and cease to be!

(AE)

1891

LITTLE MOTHER

No likeness, no picture
Remains of thee,
Little mother;
No likeness, no picture
For me to see.

No token, no sketch,
No sculpture in stone,
Little mother;
Thine image remains
In my heart alone.

o Moge ik, u
onweerdig, nooit
die beeltenis
   bederven,
Maar eerzaam laat
Zij leven in
Mij, eerzaam in
   Mij sterven.

ZONNEWENDE

Een blomken heb ik staan, nabij
   me, in de oude boekenzale,
dat altijd, naar den dag toe, keert
   zijn' blaarkes, altemale;
het wenden mag ik zus of zoo,
dat ik begere volgt het noo,
en 't zoekt, weerom naar mij gericht,
nog altijd liever 't zonnelicht!

Och, ware ik als dat blomken is,
   in al mijn doen en laten,
mijn zorgen, mijn bekommernis,
   in huis en achter straten:
't zij wat men doet of niet en doet,
't zij wat ik immer lijden moet
naar u, met herte en ziel, gericht,
o alverzettend zonnelicht!

't Is duister nu en zwaar, te mets,
   omtrent mij: oude kwalen
en nieuwe, doen, van zielgekwets,
   mij moe zijn, menigmalen,
tot dat, o God, naar U gewend,
mijn' duisterheid den dag erkent,
en ziende U, met mijne oogen dicht,
ik asem hale, in 't zonnelicht.

       *

Then, living and dying,
Be this my endeavour,
Little mother, of thee
to prove worthy
For ever and ever.

(MS)

SUNSPURGE

I have a flower standing by
me in the old library here
that at every hour will turn its rays
towards where the light appears;
my sufferance is beside the point,
it points the way it wants to point
and follows not what I'd wish done
but the liever its leader, the sun!

Might I be as that flower is,
done whatever or let slide,
in sorrow and its bitterness,
here within-doors and outside:
whatever's not or is in store, whatever I must still endure,
with heart and soul, to you I'd turn,
O light of the all-uplifting sun!

Dark it is now and lowering
round me: to the old complaints
over again come more that wring
my soul freshly as it faints,
until, O God, turning to You,
my darkness finds daylight anew,
so that I see, with eyes shut tight,
and draw breath where the sun shines bright.

(YL)

*

1892

> Tempus non erit amplius, Apoc., X, 6.

Verloren is 't gepijnd om aan den tijd,
die immer voort moet gaan
    een paal te zetten;
ja, stelt u maar en schoort u stijf,
ge 'n zult, met al uw leên en lijf,
    zijn' baan beletten.

Hij lacht met u, en, moegesold,
gij vechtend in de vore rolt,
    daar 't eeuwig varen
zijns wilden strooms voorbij u voert,
en zegepralend henenroert,
    zijn ruwe baren.

Hij stampt de hooge boomen om,
hij buigt den berg zijn' lenden krom,
    hij springt de banden
van staal intween, die vastgedaan,
bij stede en stad, hem wederstaan,
    in alle landen.

Geen wet en weet hij, noch 't en zal
hem dwingen eenig ongeval:
    geen legerbenden,
geen' wapens, geen geweld van iet
dat donderbusse of boge schiet,
    en kan hem schenden.

Onraakbaar is hij, vluchtende ooit
en vechtende; verderfnis strooit
    hij op die wilden
weêrzetten hem, 't zij burgten van
arduin gebouwd, 't zij duizend man,
    't zij duizend schilden.

1892

Tempus non erit amplius. Apoc. X, 6

We strive in vain to check the course
Of time that runs without remorse
and never alters,
We would be firm, and keep our strength
reluctant limbs submit at length,
and spirit falters.

Time mocks us as we tire and fret,
struggling and storm-beset,
where endless motion
wildly sweeps us ever on
to join the countless mortals gone
across the ocean.

It makes the mighty trees decay,
it wears the mountain-tops away;
its ruthless hand
destroys the bridges that men forge
over cataract and gorge
in every land.

It knows no law, nor turns aside,
whatever else that may betide,
No fighting band,
no weapons, no device, no lead,
from blunderbuss or crossbow sped,
can stay its hand.

Relentlessly along it goes,
and strikes us down with mortal blows,
both great and small.
The stronghold full of armed men,
No more to stand or fight again,
at last must fall.

PAUL VINCENT

't En breekt den boozen beul, van al 't
geween dat hem te voeten valt,
   geene enkele smerte,
   geen Bethlehemsche kinderdood,
   geen leêggeroofde moederschoot,
     zijn steenen herte!

Zoo moet hij varend henengaan
en al dat is aan stukken slaan,
   tot ander stonden,
   dat hij ook eens, liet licht ontzeid,
   voor eeuwig hebbe in de eeuwigheid
     zijn' dood gevonden.

1893

FIAT LUX

't Smoort, het smuikt, het smokkelwedert
   allentheen! Waar zijn ze thans,
waar de boomen, waar de huizen,
   waar de wereld, heel en gansch?

Handen uit! Wat is 't? Wat hapert
   er, genoot, dien 'k niet en zie;
die 'goedendag!' mij, uit den nevel,
   roept, van hier nen stap of drie?

Van de hooge torre en blijft er
   speur! Wat uur, hoe laat is 't wel,
aan den tijd? De zonne zie 'k niet:
   slaapt of waakt het wekkerspel?

Hier en daar een' plekke boenend,
   zit de zonne in 't duister veld;

No trace of mercy shall men meet,
who fall defeated at its feet,
Its stony heart,
for murdered babes of Bethlehem,
or mothers who gave birth to them,
shall feel no smart.

And so each day comes round again,
till everything that lives is slain,
until that hour
when tyrant Time itself shall be
swallowed in eternity
and lose its power.

(AE)

1893

FIAT LUX

Scarves of mist or doleful drizzle!
Nowhere any sign of sun;
Where are the trees and where the houses;
The world itself, where is it gone?

Hands out in front! What's what, what's moving
There? What man I cannot see
Calls out in greeting, still quite formless,
Three paces separate from me?

Now the lofty tower is hidden;
I cannot tell what is the time
By the clock or by its belfry,
For through the mist I hear no chime.

Now and then its face revealing,
Lo! The sun shows gently through,

rood, gelijk een oud versleten
stuk ongangbaar kopergeld.

Wind, waar zijt gij heengelopen?,
Ligt gij, of ievers doodgekeid,
neêrgevallen, plat ter aarde?
Wind, waar is uw roerbaarheid?

Op! Hervat uw' vluggen bezem,
vaagt des werelds wegen vrijdag
van die vale en vuile dompen:
dat het dage en daglicht zij!

Zonne, krachtig krauwt vaneen die
hoopen: ruimt uw ridderspeur;
slaat er dwers en nogmaal dwers uw'
scherpe, sterke hoeven deur!

Werpt uiteen de onvaste vlagen;
vluchten doet ze, en verre voort
zij de smoor van hier gedreven:
nevel, 's Heeren stemme aanhoort!

Fiat ha!—De zonne, ontembaar,
zegepraalt; de nevel zwicht:
onverwinlijk is de Waarheid,
onverheerbaar is het Licht!

*

't Avondt, 't avondt; traag en treurig
zinkt de zonne nederwaard;
dwijnt het licht, en gaat er geurig
reukwerk uit den roozengaard;
stille, en zonder ruit noch muit,
nijpt de nacht de dagkeerse uit.

Ruddy like a dull and tarnished
Copper coin no longer new.

Wind, where have you slipped away then?
Are you lying stricken dead,
Fallen silent down, and flattened?
Wind, we are dispirited.

Up! And wield your bustling bosom!
Wipe the heavy veils away,
Of this dark and dreary season!
Let down on us the light of day!

Sun, with mighty hoof-beats plunging,
Cleave apart these vapour trails;
Strike and strike again right through them
Till their tattered remnant fails!

Drive apart the shifting phantoms,
Make them scud away from here!
Mists obey the Lord who calls you,
Leave the whole wide vista clear.

Fiat lux! The sun, triumphant,
Makes jubilee, puts mists to flight;
Undefeated is the truth,
Crowned victorious is the light!

(AE)

*

Evening slowly veils the skies
and last puts off her western red;
the hawkmoth thrums as perfumes rise
like incense from the flower-bed,
Softly Night comes sombre-gowned
and snuffs the daylight all around.

(AE)

NAAR 'T KRIBBEKEN DES HEEREN

Naar 't kribbeken des Heeren
    Door nevel nacht en wind
Zoo komen wij ter eeren
    van 't heilig Jesukind
wij komen hem bezoeken
    en wij zij schaamle liên
het kindtjen in de doeken
    toch elk een gifte biên.

Ik geef hem eerst van allen
    met kinderlijk gevoel
voor zijnen voet gevallen
    mijn herte voor nen stoel
mijn herte en 't zij daarbinnen
    hem alles toegewijd
in 't einden en beginnen
    zoo nu zoo te allen tijd.

Ik geef hem mijne sprake
    mijn zin en mijn gedacht
Ik onderdanig make
    aan Jesus' oppermacht
geen dage en zij verleden
    geen nacht en breke er aan
dat Jesus ontevreden
    van mij moet henengaan.

Ik geef hem mijn twee handen
    mijn leden groot en kleen
en te oneer schade of schande
    en worde mij geen een
Met Jesus wil ik leven
    en sterven welgezind
den Hemel moet ons geven
    het Hemelsch Jesuskind.

THE CRIB

To the crib where lies the Lord,
This night so dark and wild,
we come to pay our homage
to the little Jesus Child.
We come like lowly shepherds,
where ass and oxen live,
to find the swaddled baby,
with nought but self to give.

Like a child I greet him
and, falling at his feet,
I give my humble heart now
to make for him a seat;
my heart and all that's in it
I offer to him here,
from very start to finish
each week, each month, each year.

I give to him my speaking;
My every thought and word
I submit to Jesus, my everlasting Lord.
No daylight shall be wasted,
nor no night following,
but I accept this baby,
heaven's eternal king.

I give him my ten fingers,
I give him every limb,
that never shall they lead me
one step away from him.
For I will live with Jesus
and perish as his friend,
and I will strive for heaven
until my life shall end.

(AE)

DE RAMEN

De ramen staan vol heiligen,
    gemiterd en gestaafd,
gemartelaard, gemaagdekroond,
    gehertoogd en gegraaid:
die 't branden van het ovenvier
    geglaasd heeft in den scherf,
die, glinsterend, al de talen spreekt
    van 't hemelboogsch geverf.

Doch schaars is herontsteken in
    den oosten het geweld
der zonnevonke, en valt zij op
    de heiligen, zoo smelt
't samijtwerk uit den mantelworp,
    de goudware uit de kroon,
en alles, even wit nu, blinkt
    en bliksemt even schoon.

Verdwenen zijt gij, hertogen
    En graven dan, zoo zaan;
Verdwenen, maagden, martelaars
    En bisschoppen: voortaan
Geen palmen, staven, stolen meer,
    't is alles henen, tot
één' helderheid gesmolten,
    in één zonnelicht – in God.

*

CHURCH WINDOW

In those high windows see the saints,
some mitred, crook in hand,
or martyred some, or holy maids,
or princes of the land,
all vitrified by furnace heat,
in every limpid hue,
as when in April days of rain
the fitful sun shines through.

Now in the east his fire, again
new-kindled straight, is felt
by that great host of serried saints;
their samite garments melt,
and all are turned to blazing white,
each drapery and fold
of cope or tabard, wimple, veil
each halo, crown of gold.

And so, before our dazzled eyes
the princes, counts, are gone,
gone too the virgins, martyrs all,
and bishops, every one;
no palms, no crooks, no stoles remain,
for all are vanished quite,
dissolved, like to the blessed saints
in God's eternal light.

(AE)

*

Spero lucem. Job, XVII, 12.

o Leeksken licht,
dat dóór het glazen dak mij
beloopen komt,
en vóór de vuisten valt:
mijn herte lust,
het langt om uw gezelschap,
en neerstig uw
bezoek genieten zal 't.

Hoe tijelijk uit
en schaarsch is uw' beleefdheid:
uw lief gelaat
hoe ras is 't mij geroofd:
ge 'n zijt nog maar
volrezen, of weêr af zijt
gij, levend licht,
gedaald en uitgedoofd!

Zijt willekom
nochtans, en, eer den nachttijd,
de vlerken los
en, leeuwerke in 't gevang,
eens vrij gepoogd
te vliegen naar het daglicht;
gezongen eens
den blijden hemelzang!

't is weêrom weg,
coch licht en is 't noch dag meer;
mijn' penne moet
voortaan wéér in den hoek:
verleene God,
die leven, licht en liefde is,
o leeksken licht,
mij morgen uw bezoek!

*

Spero lucem. Job, XVII, 12.

O Leak of light
that through the roofing glass
have leapt to me,
and fall before my feet;
my heart loves you,
it likes your company,
and duly waits
the time when we shall meet.

How timely gone
and scant is your salute;
your lovely face
how swiftly has it fled:
no sooner have you risen than you sink,

Be welcome here
though, and before night time
unloose these wings
and let me, lark in jail,
aspire once free
to fly into daylight,
singing aloud
the heaven song of hail!

It's gone again,
there's no more light or day;
my pen be put
back in the corner now:
to-morrow God,
who's life and light and love,
o leak of light,
your visit may allow!

(PC/CD)

*

Panem de Coelo ...

'k En ete niet, of 't gene ik ete,
    't heeft de dood gesmaakt;
het wreede mes, of de al zoo wreede
    hamersmete,
  heeft het afgemaakt.

Het kooren, dat de landman levend
    uit de velden voert,
wordt doodgepletterd, eer het, vleesch- en
    voedselgevend,
  mij den honger snoert.

Het doode in mij wordt levend weder,
    't vat een lijf weêr aan:
en zonder u, o dood, geen ader-
    dans en dede er
  meer mijn herte slaan.

't Gevelde rijst en wast weêromme, en,
    uit den stervensnood,
herroept ge welgevoede en versche
    levensblommen
  voor den dag, o dood!

De Godheid zelve, aan 't kruis geklonken,
    Eer 't was al volend,
ook Hij, den diepen kelk ten bodeme
    uitgedronken,
  heeft de dood gekend.

Ook Hij zou onzer zielen wezen
    eens een avondmaal
dat levend, hét alleen, genuttigd,
    zou genezen
  onze hongerkwaal.

Panem de Coelo ...

I never eat but what I eat
has by death been hit;
the cruel knife, or the as cruel
hammer beat,
slew and slaughtered it.

The corn, by farmers from the field
brought as living crop,
is crushed to death before it flesh and
may yield,
and my hunger stop.

The dead in me become alive
and with body unite;
but for you, o death, no venal
throb and drive
would my heart incite.

The felled will rise again and thrive,
and, from agony,
you call the plentiful and purest
flowers of life
forth, o death, to be!
The Lord himself, slain at the cross,
where it all must end
He too, when the deep cup was drained
to the dross,
did to death descend.

He too would for our souls once grow
to an evening meal,
which, alive, it alone, when tasted
would the woe
of our hunger heal.

o God, die, als een graan geslagen,
    vóór den vlegel vielt:
verleent, des bidde ik U, dat brood mij
    alle dagen,
    eer mijn herte ontzielt!

o God, die, als eene edel' terwe,
malsch gemalen, gingt
den oven in, aan 't kruis: en,'t brood gelijk van verwe,
daar gebraden hingt;

o Hemelmondig Manna, krachtig
inannenvoedsel, geeft
mij sterkte om eens te gaan, gestorven,
God almachtig,
daar Gij eeuwig leeft!

1894

DEN OUDEN BREVIER

Als zorgen mijn herte verslinden,
    als moedheid van 's werelds getier;
dan zoeke ik weerom den beminden,
    dan grijpe ik den ouden brevier.

o Schat ongevalschter gebeden,
    brevier, daar in 't korte geboekt,
Gods woord, en Gods wonderlijkheden,
    nooit een ongevonden en zoekt!

o 't Werk gezetelde Pausen,
    wat zegge ik, Gods eigen beworp;

o God, who slain, much like the grain,
fell before the flail;
bestow that bread on me, I pray, now
and again,
ere my heart must fail!

o God, who, like a noble wheat
mildly milled, were flung
into the furnace, to the cross, where,
baked by heat,
brown as bread you hung;

o You ambrosial Manna, mighty
manly victual, give
me strength to go one day, when dying,
God almighty,
where you ever live!

(PC/CD)

1894

THE OLD BREVIARY

When cares devour my heart's core,
and the clamour of life wearies me,
I seek out my loved one one time more,
I take my old breviary.

What a mine of prayers that ring true,
prayer book, where, brief and plain,
for God's word and God's miracles too,
one never looks in vain!

Oh, the work of the popes in their power,
no, I mean God's holy draft;

o sterkte, en als 't lijden doet flauw zijn,
    Onsterfelijk lavend geslorp!

o Weldaad wellustiger koelheid,
    o schaduwomschietende troost,
als 't vier, en de onmachtige zwoelheid,
    gestookt door den vijand, mij roost ...

Dan zuchte ... dan zit ik alleene;
    dan biede ik den booze: 'Van hier!'
dan buige en dan bidde ik, en weene ...
    dan grijp ik den ouden brevier!

HOE ZEERE VALLEN ZE AF

Hoe zeere vallen ze af,
    de zieke zomerblaren;
hoe zinken ze, altemaal,
    die eer zoo groene waren,
        te grondewaard!
Hoe deerlijk zijt gij ook
    nu, boomen al, bedegen;
hoe schamel, die weleer
    des aardrijks, allerwegen,
        de schoonste waart!

Dan valt er nog een blad;
    het wentelt, onder 't vallen,
den alderlaatsten keer,
    en 't gaat de duizendtallen
        vervoegen thans:
zoo zullen ze, een voor een
    daarin de winden bliezen
vol luider blijdzaamheid,
    nu tonge en taal verliezen,
        en zwijgen gansch.

such strength, and when pain makes me cower,
immortal, refreshing draught!

O joy so wondrously cool,
o shade-giving consolation,
when the fire and disabling passions rule,
stoked by devils to conflagration ...

Then I sit alone and sigh;
then I order the devil: 'leave me!'
then I bow and I pray and I cry,
and reach for my breviary!
(PV)

HOW SOON THEY ALL DROP DOWN

How soon they all drop down,
the leaves with sickly sheen;
they now sink, all of them,
that just now were so green,
and groundwards fall.
How pitiful you have
become now, summer trees;
how bare, that once
of earth's felicities
were fairest of all!

There falls another leaf
And as it falls gyrates –
its very final flight –
and goes to meet
the thousands of its mates:
thus they will, one by one,
the leaves through which winds have sung
in loud, exultant tones,
lose their voice and tongue –
silence complete.

Hoe zeere vallen ze af,
 onhoorbaar in de lochten,
en schier onzichtbaar, in
 de natte nevelvochten
  der droeve maand,
die 't ijzervaste speur,
 ontembaar ingetreden,
die al de onvruchtbaarheid,
 die al de onvriendelijkheden
  des Winters baant!

Daar valt er nog een blad,
 Daar nog een, uit de bogen,
Der hoogen boommenhalle,
 En 't dwerscht den onbewogen
  octobermist:

't roert geen wind, geen een,
 maar 't leken, 't leken tranen
die men gevallen zou
 uit weenende oogen wanen:
  één kerkhof is 't!

Gij, blaren, rust in vreê,
 't en zal geen een verloren,
een te kwiste gaan
 voor altijd: hergeboren,
  die nu dood zijt.
zal elk van u, dat viel,
 de zonne weêr ontwekken,
zal met uw' groenen dracht
 de groene bomen dekken,
  te zomertijd.

How soon they all drop down
noiselessly up there,
well-nigh invisible in
the damp and misty air
of the month drear
that – oh inexorable round –
begins all wild and fierce,
preparing for the bleak
and bitter winds that pierce
in winter here.

There falls another leaf,
another, from the roof
of the high hall of trees
and cuts through the aloof
October mist:

no breath of sound, not one,
yet they make one surmise
that they were tears that had
dripped from weeping eyes:
a churchyard tryst!

You leaves, rest now in peace,
you'll not be lost, no fear,
not one will go to waste,
but, resurrected here,
you who now have died,
each one of you that fell,
the sun will wake you up,
will with your green attire
cover the green trees up
at summertide.

O Zomer!... Ik zal eens
    ook Adams zonde boeten
gevallen en verdord
    in 's winters grafsteê, moeten;
    maar, 's levens geest,
dien gij gesteken hebt
    in mijn gestorven longen,
dien zult gij mij voor goed
    niet laten afgedwongen,
    die 't graf ontreest!

1895

SLAPENDE BOTTEN

Ten halven afgewrocht,
ontvangen, niet geboren;
    gevonden, algeheel,
noch algeheel verloren,
    zoo ligt er menig rijm
onvast in mij, en beidt
    den aangenamen tijd
van volle uitspreekbaarheid

    Zoo slaapt de botte in 't hout,
Verdonkerd en verdoken;
    Geen blomme is er ooit,
geen blad eruit gebroken;
    maar blad en blomme en al,
het ligt erin, en beidt
    den dag, den dageraad ...
de barensveerdigheid.

Oh summer! ... One day I'll
pay too for Adam's sin,
fallen, shrivelled up
a wintry grave enter in;
but life's breath that You gave,
that You instilled
in my lungs' mortality,
you will not let that be
wrested for good from me,
who'll rise up from the grave.

(PV)

1895

SLEEPING BUDS

Performed imperfectly,
conceived, not duly born;
not found entirely,
entirely not forlorn
thus lies many a rhyme
biding, unripe in me,
the pleasurable time
of speakability.

Thus sleep the bushes' buds,
recondite and concealed;
no flower yet unfurled,
no leaf till now revealed;
but leaf and flower lie,
embedded, eagerly
biding the day, the dawn ...
the full parturiency.

(PC/CD)

1896

CASSELKOEIEN

    Aanschouwt mij, hier en daar,
      die bende Casselkoeien,
        die, louter bruin van haar,
        als zoovel blommen bloeien,
in 't gers en in de zon, die, zinkend henentiet:
die, rood, het roode veld vol roode vonken giet.

      't Is prachtig overal,
        't prachtig, hoe de huiden
          dier koeien liefgetal
        van vouwe en verwen luiden:
't prachtig, hoe ze staan, gebeiteld en gesneên,
lijk beelden, over heel die wijde weide heen.

      Daar zijnder, roode als vier;
        Castanjebruin geboende;
          Naar donkerbaaide bier,
        Naar bijkans zwart bier doende;
beglinsterd en beglansd: van vel en verwigheid,
gelijk en ongelijk, -terwijl de zonne beidt.

      Al langzaam langer speelt,
        Dwersdeur de weidegronden,
          't zij welker koe een beeld
        van schaduw bijgebonden;
en, wangedrochtig groot, in 't donker gers, voortaan,
zie 'k zwarte spoken van gevlerkte koeien staan.

      Goên nacht! De zonne beet
        Ten neste neêr: tot morgen
          is al dat verwe heet
        en oogen aast, verborgen:
De koeien zijn voorbij, gedelgd en uitgedoofd,
en ... morgen weêr, ontwekt ze 't blinkend zonnehoofd.

1896

THE CASSEL COWS

The Cassel cows stand gazing
As I slowly pass,
Their glossy brown coats gleaming
Like flowers in the grass,
In the ruddy light of the slowly setting sun
That sheds his fiery rays over the burnished plain.

Glorious it is on all sides,
And glorious it is to see
The lining tints in the creases
Of the gentle creatures' hides,
As scattered in groups, the cows silhouetted against the sky,
Stand out like carven images in the fields, as I pass by.

Some are chestnut brown,
Some are red as fire,
Others deep red brown,
Almost like black beer.
Polished and shining are they all; in colour and texture,
Alike and yet unlike; meanwhile the sun lingers.

The longer he tarries thus,
His transverse beams are thrown
Across the plain over the cows,
Whose shadows now have grown
Into monster phantom shapes, which in the grass appear
Like the sable-winged ghosts of cattle standing there.

Good night! The sun descends
Into his bed in the West;
Until dawn, all that glow
And magic is at rest,
The cows are seen no more, having disappeared from view
Until to-morrow, when the sun shall rise anew. (MS)

HIER BEN IK

    O groote God,
    in het sterrenheer
herkenbaar uit der maten,
    'n wilt, die maar
    een mugge en ben,
een zandeken, mij laten!

    Het middent al
    terug naar U,
't gewordene uit Uw' handen;
    en toornend houdt
    Gij alles in,
't onmijdbare Uwer banden.

    Uw eigendom
    is al hetgeen
Gij, dagelijks of zelden,
    Als leenheere, in
    Mijn handen zet;
't is 't Uwe, en 'k wille 't gelden.

    U manschap doen
    Naar ridders recht
En eere, is mij betamen,
    En nooit zal 'k
    Mij Uw, o God,
Diens schild ik drage, schamen.

    Hier ben ik, Uw
    Ontbiên getrouw
Slaan anderen, verwaten,
    Den aweg in,
    'k wille, o goede,
o groote God, U laten!

HERE AM I

Almighty God,
the starry host
shines forth at your command.
What then of me,
poor puny fly,
mere particle of sand?

All things obey
your sovereign will,
created by your Word.
You bid them be –
they one and all
acknowledge You their Lord.

To your domain
all things belong
which, many times or few,
You chose to give,
or take from me;
I pledge them all to you.

Your henchman, I,
your faithful knight.
You, liege lord, I acclaim.
May nought that I
may ever do
upon my shield bring shame.
So here am I
To do your will.
Though others fall away.
I never shall,
so help me, Lord,
allow my steps to stray.

(AE)

PAUL VINCENT

WINTERMUGGEN

De wintermuggen zijn
    aan 't dansen, ommentomme,
zoo wit als muldersmeel,
    zoo wit als molkenblomrne.

Ze varen hooge, in 't vloe;
    ze dalen diepe, in de ebbe:
ze weven, heen en weêr,
    hun' witte winterwebbe.

Hun' winterwebbe zal,
    dat lijnwaad zonder vlekken,
den zuiverlijkein schoot
    van moeder Aarde dekken.

Ze ligt in heuren slaap,
    ze droomt den schuldeloozen,
den maagdelijken droom
    van nieuwe lenteroozen.

Ze ligt in heuren slaap,
    ze droomt den wonderbaren,
den liefelijken droom
    van 's zomers harpenaren.

Ze ligt in heuren droom,
    ze droomt van overvloed en
van voorspoed overal,
    om vee en volk en voeden.

'n Wekt ze niet,'n laat
    heur geen geruchte dwingen,
om, al te schier ontwekt,
    uit heuren slaap te springen!

WINTER MIDGES

The winter midges are
a-whirling, dancing dots,
as white as miller's meal,
as white as curdling clots.

They're flying high, in flood;
they're dropping deep, in ebb;
they're weaving, up and down,
their whitest winterweb.

Their winterweb will now,
a linen without stain,
upon the maiden lap
of mother Earth remain.

She lies and slumbers on,
she dreams the innocent,
the virgin reverie
of roses renaissant.

She lies and slumbers on,
she's dreaming the sublime,
the lovely reverie
of harpers' summertime.

She lies and slumbers on,
she dreams of plenitude
and of prosperity,
for folk and flock and food.

Don't wake her, let her not
by any sound be pressed,
lest she, too soon awake,
should start up from her rest!

Daar ligt ze nu en rust:
    Heur zwijgend beddelaken,
de wintermuggen spree'n 't,
    die geen geruchte en maken.

Ze draaien op en af
    en af en op en omme,
zoo wit als melk, als meel,
    als molke en runselblomme.

TRANEN

    't Is nevelkoud,
  en 's halfvoornoens, nog
duister in de lanen;
    de boomen, die 'k
  nog nauwlijks zien kan,
weenen dikke tranen.

    't En regent niet,
  maar't zeevert ... van die
fijngezichte, natte
    schiervatbaarheid,
  die stof gelijkt, en
wolke en wulle en watte.

    't Is aschgrauw al,
  beneên, omhooge, in
't veld en langs de lanen:
    de boomen, die 'k
  nog nauwlijks zien kan,
weenen dikke tranen.

There now she lies and sleeps
Without a sound her bed
is with the silent sheets
of winter midges spread.

They're turning up and down
And down and up, these dots,
As white as milk, as meal,
As cream and curdling clots.

(PC/CD)

TEARS

'T is damply cold,
mid-morning mist still
dim in every lane;
the trees, which I
can scarcely see, are
weeping tears of pain.

It does not rain,
it slavers ... such a
shivered, vapoury
near-palpability
as dust and
down and drapery.

'T is ashy grey,
beneath, aloft, in
every field and lane:
the trees, which I
can scarcely see are
weeping tears of pain.

(PC/CD)

1897

JAM SOL RECEDIT

Heel 't Westen zit gekibbelkappeld,
    Gewaggelwolkt, al hil en dal;
't zit blauw en groen en geluw g'appeld;
    te morgen nog volstormde 't al,
en stille is't nu! De zonne, aan 't zinken,
doet hier en daar een splete blinken,
    en kijkt erdeure, nu en dan.
Heel 't westen bleust en blinkt ervan ...
Zoo heerlijk is't, als of er zoude
een reuzeinpenning, rood van goude,
    den reuzenspaarpot vallen in
    der slapengaande zeevorstin.

1897

IAM SOL RECEDIT

The entire west is curdle-clotted,
full flocculence, sheer hill and vale;
it's blue and green and yellow dotted;
this morning rushed with storm and gale,
and now it's calm! The sun, in sinking,
sets here and there a crevice blinking,
through which, from time to time, it winks.
The entire west thus blushing blinks ...
Being as glorious to behold
as some giant red coin of gold
that in the giant purse has been
dropt of the ocean's sleepy queen.

(PC/CD)

TWEE HORSEN

Ze stappen, hun' bellen al klinken,
    De vrome twee horsen te gaar;
Ze zwoegen, ze zweeten; en blinken
    Doet 't blonde gelijm van hun haar.

Ze stappen, ze stenen, ze stijven
    De stringen; en 't ronde gareel,
Het spant op hun' spannende lijven:
    De voerman beweegt ze aan een zeel.

De wagen komt achter. De rossen,
    Gelaten in 't lastig geluid
Der schokkende, bokkende bossen,
    Gaan stille en gestadig, vooruit.

Geen zwepe en behoort er te zinken,
    Geen snoer en genaakt er één haar:
Zoo stappen, hun' bellen al klinken,
    De vrome twee horsen, te gaar.

TWA AIVERS**

As they trot wi' a' thir bells jinglin,
The twa bainlie badgets thegither
Come pechan an' papplan, sweit leamin
Atwish the roan lowe o' the mane.

Breath steamin, they amble; an' strainin
The hamsticks, the round tackle streeks
Athort the breid o' thir heavin breists,
The wagoner gafferin at the reins.

The wain comes adreight as the aivers,
Dreean the waesome skirl an' skriegh
O' the rackety, bickerin nave,
Peaceably, wi' steady pace, advance.

Oan awther spauld ye'll hear nae whip fa',
Nae bridle-dunt as skelps a hair,
As they trot wi' a' thir bells jinglin,
The twa bainlie badgets baith ane.

** This poem is particularly marked by dialect forms and specialised rural vocabulary unfamiliar to the town-born. What Gezelle was attempting to create was a literary language based on (West) Flemish dialect similar to Lallans, the synthetic variety of Scots pioneered by Hugh MacDiarmid and others at a later date. Such a poem does not translate convincingly into English. Moreover, a Scots version gives an English reader the same sensation of oddness that a reader of standard Dutch feels when faced with Gezelle's original. He will, however, need this glossary: Twa – two; aiver – workhorse; bainlie – big-boned, sturdy; badget – workhorse; thegither – together; pechan an' paplan – panting and heated; leam – gleam; atwish – between; lowe – flame; hamstick – part of the collar to which harness is attached; streek – stretch; athort – across; breid – breadth; gaffer – direct; adreight – behind; dree – endure; waesome – woeful; skirl an' skreigh – scream and shriek; bicker – clatter; nave – wheel-hub; awther – either; spauld – shoulder, the breadth of back between; dunt – blow; skelp – strike; baith ane – together.
(YL)

BONTE ABEELEN

WIT als watte, en teenegader
groen, is 't bonte abeelgeblader.

Wakker, als een wekkerspel,
wikkelwakkelwaait het snel.

Groen vanboven is 't en zonder
minke, wit als melk, vanonder.

Onstandvastig volgt het, gansch,
't onstandvastig windgedans.

Wisselbeurtig, op en neder,
slaat liet, als een' vogelveder.

Wit en grauw, zoo, dóór de lucht,
'bonte-abeelt' de duivenvlucht.

WINTERSTILTE

   Een witte spree
    ligt overal
gespreid op 's werelds akker;
   geen mensche en is,
    men zeggen zou,
geen levend herte wakker.

   Het vogelvolk,
    Verlegen en
verlaten, in de takken
    des perebooms
    te piepen hangt,
daar niets en is te pakken!

THE ASPEN TREE

White and green together heaves
The aspen all its glancing leaves.

Ever awake, like a ticking cloek,
To and fro its branches rock.

From above, it is all a shimmer of green,
And milk-white when from below it is seen.

Most unpeaceable of trees,
It dances with the fitful breeze.

Up and down in windy weather
Wave its leaves, like a bird's feather.

White and grey it gleams in the night,
Like a flock of doves in flight.

(JBi)

WINTER QUIET

As far as eyes
Can reach, there lies
A sheet of white that glistens ...
Far, far around No breath, no sound ...
The ear to silence listens ...

The birds are chill,
And sit so still,
Upon the pear-tree perching ...
The snow lies thick,
There's nought to pick,
No crumb nor worm for their searching.

'''t Is even stille
en stom, alhier
aldaar; en, ondertusschen,
en hoore ik maar
het kreunen meer,
en 't kriepen, van de musschen.

GIERZWALUWEN (Cypselus Apus)

Zie, zie, zie,
zie! zie! zie!
zie!! zie!! zie!!
zie!!!'
tieren de
zwaluwen,
twee-driemaal
drie,
zwierende en
gierende:
'Niemand, die ...
die
bieden den
stiet ons zal!
Wie, wie? wie??
wie???'

Piepende en
kriepende,
zwak en ge-
zwind;
haaiende en
draaiende
rap als de
wind;
wiegende en
vliegende
vlug op de

No voice is heard,
No beak of bird
Startles the brooding quiet ...
But listen now!
On yonder bough
The hungry sparrows riot!
(JBi)

SWIFTS (Cypselus Apus)

See, see, see,
see! see! see!
see!! see!! see!!
see!!!'
hear hear these
weeping swifts
twice or thrice
three,
sweeping and:
weeping there:
'Do we see ...
see
anyone
we can't flee'?
We, we? we??
we???

Peeping and
cheeping, lithe
and disci-
plined;
wheeling and reeling as
quick as the
wind;
lifting and
drifting so
swift on the

PAUL VINCENT

    vlerk,
spoeien en
roeien ze
ringsom de
    kerk.

Leege nu
Zweven ze, en
geven ze
    bucht;
hooge nu
hemelt hun'
vlerke, in de
    lucht:
amper nog
hoore ik ... en,
die 'k niet en
    zie,
lijvelijk
zingen ze:
'Wie??? wie?? wie?
    Wie ...'

OP KRUKKEN

Waarom, waarom
en wete ik niet,
het kwelt mij, al
    te onzelden,
een zwarigheid,
die 'k nooit en kan,
wat poge ik doe,
    vermelden.

wing,
going and
rowing round
spires they
swing.

Down they are
gliding, soon
widening their
flight;
skyward are
waving their
wings in the
height:
scarcely I
hear these ... I
no longer
see,
singing still
vividly:
'We??? we?? we?
We ... '

(PC/CD)

YEARNING

O why, O why?
o do not know
Why sorrow comes
So often,
A heaviness
That will not ease,
A pang no balm
can soften;

Daar hapert iets
aan ziele, aan lijf,
aan bei misschien
    te zamen,
daarvan ik dit
noch dat en weet
beseffelijk
    te namen.

Als 't avond is,
't zou middag of
't zou morgen zijn
    mij moeten;
als 't morgent weêr,
of noent, 't en geeft
mij geen, of kleen,
    verzoeten.

't Is winter: 'Of
het zomer ware,
of lang en schoon
    de dagen!'
Des zomers: 'Ach,
hoe lange ik naar ...
hoe lusten miij
    de vlagen!'

't Verdriet mij, in
de steê, en 'k ga
te lande, om lust
    en leven.
Te lande: 't Doet
mij deugd in stad,
och, ware ik daar
    gebleven!'

A falling short –
In body? Soul?
In both, it seems,
Together;
A thing whose name
Eludes my tongue
For ever and
For ever.

When evening comes
I would it were
The afternoon
Or morning;
When noonday comes
Or failing light,
I would the day
Were dawning.

In winter, O!
Or summer-time,
The long, the sun-
Lit hours!
In summer, o!
My Soul is full
Of howling winds
and showers.

How wearily
In city streets
I seek the restful field!
But once away,
I straight return;
O where shall I be healed?

Ze komen en
ze zoeken en
ze vinden mij,
    de dezen,
daar verre ik van
begere, en bij
geen zulke meer,
    te wezen.

Alleene en is 't
niet houdelijk:
'Och, mochte ik mij
    één vinden,
die 't kluwen van
mijn herte hielp
mij, heel en al,
    ontwinden!'

Als alles mij
te monde gaat
en meê, naar mijn
    verlangen,
dan is het, dat
ik, lui en lam
en lusteloos,
    blijf hangen.

Waarom liet is
en wete ik niet,
noch hoe het is
    en wete ik:
maar dat het is,
en lastig is,
om lijdene, 'n
    vergete ik!

Where people come
To seek me out?
By why, alas,
They only,
Whose presence frets
My troubled soul
Which rather would be lonely?

But when, alone,
I face this self I
Am for ever
Fleeing,
Where find one soul
To bring a salve
To my so troubled
Being?

If all I seek
One day should seem
In every way
Perfected,
't there and then
that listelessly
I drag my feet
Dejected.

Why this should be
I do not know,
My days with rue
Besetting,
But so it is,
And I must bear
A heart-ache past
Forgetting.

't En helpt al niet
te zitten en
te snuisteren
    in boeken;
't en zij voor dit
mijn ongemak
geen kruidekens
    te zoeken.

't Moet ievers iets,
onvindbaar nu
toch vindbaar zijn
    mij, mensche;
die, half verzaad,
her, altijd her,
geheel verzaad
    mij wensche.

't Zal beter, als
de spa gevraagd
is, eenmaal, ééns
    gelukken:
naar hooger goed
als wereldsch goed,
hier springen ...
    op krukken.

I find no ease
And vainly seek
For solace in
My reading.
There is no herb,
For all. I seek,
To staunch my spirit's
Bleeding.

Somewhere must be,
Not yet revealed,
A fire for ever
burning
to satisfy
the heart's desire
and answer every
yearning.

Dig deep the hole,
wipe clean the spade,
the spade the sexton
clutches,
and I shall limp
the world no more
when cast away
my crutches.

(AE)

JUVABIT!

Geeft aan beter herte als 't mijne,
zoo in 't zeggene als in 't zijne,
　dit mijn, rel- en rijmgepoog
nu een dropke en dan een dropke,
nu een klopke en dan een klopke,
　maakt het iemands ooge ondroog,
iemands herte een beter herte
iemands smerte een minder smerte,
　van die 't lezen, altegaar,
　heden, morgen, hier of daar,
troost den armen dichter geven
zal 't, in dit en 't ander leven!

　　　　*

Jordane van mijn hert
en aderslag mijns levens,
　O Leye, o vlaamsche vloed,
　lijk Vlaanderen onbekend;
hoe overmachtigt mij
de mate uws vreugdegevens,
　wanneer ik sta en schouwe
　uw' vrijen boord omtrent!

Hoe vaart gij welgemoed,
de malsche meerschen lavend
　met blijder vruchtbaarheid,
　te Scheldewaard, en voort
ten Oceaan, u, zelf,
een' diepe vore gravend,
　die 't oude en vrij land
　van Vlaanderen toebehoort.

Wat zijt ge schoone, o Leye,
als 't helderblauwe laken

COMFORT

Comfort better hearts than mine,
heal their hurt with oil and wine,
whisper solace in their ears,
now a droplet, then a droplet,
falling in a gentle couplet,
offering release in tears.
Mend a broken heart again,
Make the pain a lesser pain.
For, whoever, maybe, reads me,
If such a thing indeed may be,
I will cease to be downcast,
Now and when earth's life is past.

(AE)

*

Oh, Jordan of my heart,
whose pulse through my life pounds,
O Leie, Flemish stream,
like Flanders, still unknown:
it overwhelms me quite,
your bounty without bounds,
as I now stand and watch
on your free bank, alone!

You flow benevolently,
and lush fields fed you keep
with joyous fruitfulness,
towards the River Scheldt, and then
on to the Sea itself,
digging a furrow deep,
part of the old, free land
that makes up Flanders' fen.

How fair you are, o Leie,
When the bright blue sheet

der hemeletente wijd
en breed is uitgespreid,
en dat, uit heuren throon,
de felle zunne, aan 't blaken,
 vertweelingt heur gezichte
 in uwe blauwigheid!

Dan leeft het rondom al
uw' groengezoomde kanten,
 aanzijds en heraanzijds,
 zoo verre ik henenschouw,
van lieden, die weêrom,
en nu in 't water, planten
 den overjaarschen bloei
 van hunnen akkerbouw.

Den bast, die, onlangs, toen
hij jong was, jong en schoone,
 't gezicht verblijdde, maar
 één levend legtapijt;
die, veel te lichte, eilaas!
De blauwe maagdenkroone
 verloos, en bleef het lieve
 en jeugdig leven kwijt!

Het vlas! Nu staat 't gedoopt,
Jordane, in uw lanken,
 gegord in haveren stroo,
 dat banden gouds gelijkt;
bij duizend duizenden
van bonden, die vier planken
 bewaren, ketenvast
 en aan den wal gefijkt.

Hoe zucht gij, om weêr uit
dit stovend bad te komen;
 Hoe zucht gij, zoo de ziel,

Of the heavens' tent is
spread wide and broad,
and when, from on its throne,
the fierce sun, breathing heat,
doubles its countenance
in your azure bed!

Then it comes to life
around your green-fringed edge,
on this side and on yon,
as far as I can see,
with folk, who now again
down in the water wedge
the ripe and bounteous yield
of their industry.

The bark, which just now, when
it was young, young and fair,
delighted the eye, is now
a living mosaic
that, far too soon, alas,
lost its blue virgin
crown, and its rare
young life did forsake!

The flax! Now it is soaked,
O Jordan, twixt your flanks,
bound in oaten straw
that looks like a golden band;
thousands upon thousands
of sheaves, hemmed by four planks,
and shackled fast
and with posts kept close to land.

How you sigh, to leave
this steaming bath again;
you sigh, just like the soul,

  de vrome kerstene, doet,
die, na gedulde pijn,
vol hopen en vol schromen,
  verlangt het licht te zien
  dat haar verlossen moet!

Verdraagt den harden steen
nog wat, die, korts nadezen,
  gelicht, u helpen zal
  ter vrijheid; en de dood,
die u gedwongen hield,
zal zelf gedwongen wezen,
  u latende uit het graf
  en uit de Leyeschoot.

Die steen heeft u gedempt,
g'ootmoedigd en gedoken,
  tot dat uw taaie rug,
  gemurruwd en verzaad,
geen weêrstand biên en zou
aan hem die u, gebroken,
  tot lijn hermaken zal
  en edel vlasgewaad.

Hoe krielt het wederom,
langs al de Leyeboorden,
  van lieden, half gekleed,
  die half in 't water staan,
en halen, lekende uit,
lijk lijken van versmoorden,
  't gebonden, zappig vlas,
  en 't spreidende openslaan!

t Verrijst! Het wordt alhier,
het wordt aldaar bewogen,
  gestuikt, gekeuveld en
  gehut. De zonne lacht

the pious Christian sighs
who, after suffering,
in hope, but scared of pain,
longs to see the light,
so it from sin can rise!

Endure the heavy stone
a little, you'll soon come out!
Raised, it will help you up
to freedom; and death's doom,
that kept you in its thrall,
will then be put to rout,
freeing you from the grave
and from the Leie's womb.

That stone had pressed you down,
humbled you and sunk you
until your sturdy back,
softened and soaked quite through,
would offer no resistance
to one who tried to crush you,
to turn you into linen
and fine flax fabric too.

It teems on Leie's banks
once more and all around
with people, half-undressed,
in water to their thighs,
and hauling, soaking wet,
like corpses of the drowned,
the bound and soaking flax,
spreading it so it dries!

It rises up! It's moved here
and chucked there
into sheaves and portions and
stacks. The sunlight laughs

'en speelt in 't droogend schif,
dat, 't water uit gezogen,
    heur fijne stralen drinkt
    en fijndere verruwpracht!

Wat zie 'k! o Israël,
lijk in de bibelprenten,
    geldeend, den overtocht
    van 't Abrahamse diet;
gesmaldeeld en geschaard,
in lijnwaadgrauwe tenten,
    ontelbaar, zoo 't den dwang
    van Pharao verliet!

Beloofde land van god,
Jordane, in 't hooge Noorden,
    hoe schoon 't gelegerd volk,
    dat, God gehoorzaam, voet
en hand te zamen, zwoegt
naar uwaard, en de boorden
    van 't stroomend waterkleed
    strijdmachtig leven doet!

Ik hef, lijk Bala'am,
mijn woord op, en 'k bezegen
    den arbeidweerden troost
    dien 't neerstig Vlanderen vand.
Zij 't immer God getrouw,
God dankbaar, God genegen,
    en weerd de diere kroon
    die hem de vrijheid spant,

    Zoo lang de Leye loopt,
    zoo lang de velden dragen

and plays on the drying clay
that from the water sucked
drinks in its delicate rays
and glorious coloured draughts!

What do I see! o Israel,
as in the Bible prints,
in miniature, the crossing
of Abraham's own folk,
divided into troops –
tent canvas in grey tints –
countless, when they fled
great Pharaoh's yoke!

Promised Land of God,
Jordan, far up north,
How fair the army is
that, God, obedient toils
with hands and feet,
towards you struggles forth,
so that the watery bank
with work and energy boils!

I raise, like Balaam did,
my voice up, and I bless
the industrious consolation
that toiling Flanders found ...!
May it stay loyal to God,
be God's in faithfulness
and worth the precious freedom
with which its head is crowned,

as long as Leie flows,
as long as fields still bear

    den taaien lijnwaadoost,
    die op heur boorden groeit;
Zoo lang 't gestorven vlas
herleeft in kant en kragen,
    en, sneeuwit, op de borst
    van jonk- en schoonheid bloeit!

*

Klopt het om de Messe,
luistert naar mijn lesse:
Toebak zegt en Bier
zeere, weg van hier!

Ik ben baas, en wilt gij, gasten,
's zondags naar uw pinte tasten
als de klokke roept, komt aan,
ik ben bass en gij zult gaan.

Als de Pastorsklokke klipt,
elkeen naar de Messe wipt;
of, die willen blijven pekken,
'k zal ze bij de krage stekken.

their hardy linen race
that grows upon its side;
while the flax that's dead
revives in ruffs and lace
and, snow-white, blossoms forth
young, pretty breasts to hide!

(PV)

*

The church calls us all to mass!
So therefore put aside your glass;
Leave your baccy and your beer;
These things have no business here.

I am boss, and if you think
Sunday morning is for drink,
Listen to what the bells now say:
'We are boss and you obey!'

When your pastor's churchbell tolls,
Let it reach into your souls,
And if you find this not enough,
I will take you by the scruff!

(AE)

IN SPECULO

    Hoe kan dat zijn,
o Schepper van hierboven,
      dat ik U maar
   en zie als in een' glans;
    als in een glas,
te zelden onbestoven
     van doom en stof.
  en nooit geheel en gansch?

    Zoo Gij bestaat,
en God zijt, moet het wezen,
     dat ik U zie,
  dat, zonder doek, entwaar,
    ik schouwen kan,
en, schouwende, in 't nadezen,
     van bij U zie
   en eeuwig op U staar!

    Hoe kan dat zijn:
om niet en is gegeven,
     uit uwe hand,
het leefvermogen, dat
    mij zuchten doet,
en zoeken, naar een leven,
    dat alle goed,
in 't zien van U, bevat!

   Daar komt toch eens,
ten oosten uit, een dagen,
    een dageraad,
eene eeuwigheid, die niet
   meer weg en kan
noch weder, noch vertragen
    het zielgezucht,
dat zoekt en niet en ziet.

IN SPECULO

How can it be,
Creator there aloft,
That I should see
You but as a glint;
As in a glass,
Too obfuscated oft
With damp and dust:
And never quite distinct?

If You exist
And are God, it must be
That I see You;
That, withour cloth, somewhere
You are looked on,
That, looking, finally,
I see You near
And always at You stare!

Hoe can it be:
Not vainly have You given,
By your mild hand,
The vital aptitudes
that make me strive,
and sigh after a living,
that all the good,
by seeing you includes!

Once there will come
From orient a day
A dawning and
A diurnity
That cannot fade
Away nor lead astray
The striving soul,
Which seeks and does not see.

        Mijne ooge zal
eens vol U zien, en varen
       zoo 't druppeiken
   in zee, dat is versmoord:
      zij zal U zien,
verafgrond in de baren
       der ziende zee,
  die bedde en heeft noch boord!

1898

EGO FLOS ...
                    CANT. II

    Ik ben een blomme
En bloeie vóór uwe oogen,
   Geweldig zonnelicht,
   Dat, eeuwig onontaard,
   Mij, nietig schepselken,
In 't leven wilt gedoogen
   En na dit leven, mij
   Het eeuwig leven spaart.

    Ik ben een blomme
En doe des morgens open,
   Des avonds toe mijn blad,
   Om beurtelings, nadien,
   Wanneer gij, zonne, zult,
Heropgestaan, mij nopen,
   Te ontwaken nog eens of
   Mijn hoofd den slaap te biên.

     Mijn leven is
Uw licht: mijn doen, mijn derven,
   Mijn hope, mijn geluk

My eye will see
You wholly once and craves
To be the drop
That in the ocean sank:
It will see You,
While swallowed by the waves,
That seeing sea
With neither bed nor bank!

(PC/CD)

1898

EGO FLOS ...
                    (Cant. II, 1)

I am a flower
and bloom before your eyes,
O mighty blazing sun,
steadfast eternally,
who'll spare me, creature, in
my little earthly life,
and will hereafter grant me
life in eternity.

I am a flower,
and in the morning open,
at eve I close my leaf,
so that alternately,
whenever you, o sun,
will rise again and stir me,
I may awake once more
or yield my head to sleep.

My life is in
your light: my work, my wanting,
my hope, my happiness,

Mijn éénigste en mijn al;
Wat kan ik, zonder u,
Als eeuwig, eeuwig sterven;
Wat heb ik, zonder u,
Dat ik beminnen zal?

'k ben ver van u,
ofschoon gij, zoete bronne
van al wat leven is
of immer leven doet,
mij naast van al genaakt
en zendt, o lieve zonne,
tot in mijn diepste diep
uw aldoorgaanden gloed.

Haalt op, haalt af!...
Ontbindt mijne aardsche boeien;
ontwortelt mij, ontdelft
mij ...! Henen laat mij ... laat
daar 't altijd zomer is
en zonnelicht mij spoeien
en daar gij, eeuwige, ééne,
alschoone blomme, staat.

Laat alles zijn
voorbij, gedaan, verleden
dat afscheid tusschen ons
en diepe kloven spant;
laat morgen, avond, al
dat heenmoet, heenetreden,
laat uw oneindig licht
mij zien, in 't Vaderland!

Dan zal ik vóór ...
o nee, niet vóór uwe oogen
maar naast u, nevens u,
maar in u bloeien zaan;

my only and my all;
what is there, without you,
but ever, ever dying,
what have I, without you
to love with all my soul?

I'm far from you,
although you, sweetest spring
of everything that lives
or from which life does flow,
yet come so close to me
and send, o dearest sun,
into my deepest deep
your all-pervading glow.

Lift up, undo! ...
untie my earthly fetters;
uproot me, and unearth me! ...
hence, o let me, there
where always summer reigns
and sunlight let me hasten,
and where, eternal, one,
all-fairest flower, you stand.

Let all the things
be past, and gone, departed,
that still divide us now,
like chasms between us stand;
let morning, evening, all
that's fleeting, flee now from me,
let me your endless light
behold, in Heaven's land!

Then I'll before ...
o, not before your eyes,
but by you, near to you,
but in you blossom soon;

zoo gij mij schepselken,
in 't leven wilt gedoogen;
zoo in uw eeuwig licht
mij gij laat binnengaan!

    *

'k En hoore u nog niet,
o nachtegale. En
de paaszunne zit
    in 't oosten;
waar blijft gij zoo lange,
of hebt gij misschien
vergeten van ons
    te troosten?

't Zomert, 't is waar,
't en loovert, 't en lijdt
geen bladtje nog uit
    de hagen;
't zit ijs in de wind,
't zit sneeuw in de lucht,
't stormen, dat 't doet,
    en vlagen.

Toch spreeuwt het en vinkt
het luide, overal;
de merelaan lacht
    en tatelt;
het muscht en het meest,
het koekoet, in 't hout;
het zwaluwt en 't zwiert
    en 't swatelt.

Waar blijft gij zoo lang,
de nachtgale; en

if in that life you'll let
me, creature, have my being,
if your eternal light
you'll let me enter then.

(TW)

*

I cannot hear you yet,
o nightingale, and
the Easter sun waits in the east;
what's kept you so long,
or have you perhaps
forgotten how to
bring peace?

Summer's not here yet, it's true,
no leaves sprout, no green
shoots out of
the hedgerow;
there's ice in the wind,
there's snow in the air,
there are storms all about
and the wind gusts blow.

Yet there's starlings and finches,
loud everywhere;
the blackbird laughs
and clatters,
it sparrows and tits,
it cuckoos in the wood;
it swallows and swifts
and it chatters.

What's kept it so long,
the nightingale; does

PAUL VINCENT 217

vergeet hij van ons
    te troosten?
't En zomert nog niet,
maar zomeren zal 't:
de Paaschzunne zit
    in 't oosten.

SLAAPLIED

Waait mij nu zoetjes,
    O zuchtende wind:
Wiegt mij en douwt mij
    Dat zuilende kind;
Speelt om zijn wichtelijk
    Aanzichtje en laat
Jesuken rusten: het
    Slapen nu gaat.

Palmen, die roerende en
    wagende zijt,
stilt om mijn kindeke uw
    takken nen tijd
engelkes, zoetjes, ach,
    Jesuken wilt
Slapen: uw' tonge en
    Uw' harpe nu stilt.

Vogelkes, zwijgt, die daar
    Huppelt en springt;
Dauwdruppels, zoetjes, en
    Belt noch en klinkt;
Zonne, uwe machtige
    Stralen verfrischt:
't kindeken Jesus ... in
    slape ... nu is 't!

it forget to bring
us peace?
Summer's not here yet,
but summer will come:
the Easter sun waits in the east.

(PV)

CHRISTMAS LULLABY

O wayward wind
let your breath be mild and
rock me the cradle
of Jesus, my child.
Softly over
his eyelids play
until in slumber he slips away.

Reeds that over
the waters bow,
keep your stems
from clashing now.
Angels be
most careful lest
your tongues and harps
disturb his rest.

Birdies, you
may flutter and spring,
but, lest you wake him,
do not sing.
Shades of evening,
growing deep,
see my babe
fall – asleep.

(AE)

VOORBIJ ...

Voorbij ...
is, eer, het woord voluit
mijn tonge ontvalt, het vlerkgeluid
des vogels die al dorpen wijd
van hier is, haast in géénen tijd.

Voorbij,
zoo vaart het stoomgetuig,
met vier- en vonk- en rookgespuig,
de schenen af, één stonde, en is
verdwenen in de duisternis.

Voorbij,
zoo zie 'k de schaduw langs
de stappen gaan mijns wandelgangs,
en schielijk al 't nieuw akkergroen,
gemeten verre, in 't donker doen.

Voorbij,
zoo vaagt een striepken licht
de valsterre over 't aangezicht
des nachts; en ik ... 'k en zie daarvan
geen speur, eer zesse ik tellen kan.

Voorbij,
o God, u uitgespaard,
gaat alles heen- en tendenwaard;
gaat al dat is of was voorbij:
gij zijt alleene en blijft God, gij!

TO...?

It's gone!
As scarce the words are said,
a bird has started up and sped
across the fields in wing-clap flight
and now already slips from sight.

It's gone!
Soon swallowed by the dark,
with all her flame and smoke and spark,
a steam train thunders through the night
till sight and sound are vanished quite.

It's gone!
The shadows longer grow
around my footsteps as I go,
until they brim the countryside,
and all is darkened far and wide.

It's gone!
A sudden streak of light
shoots across the face of night;
it fades away to nought before
a man can count from one to four.

It's gone!
All things God made must tend
sooner, later, to an end.
Everything must pass away,
only God unchanging stay.

(AE)

AAN ...?

Gelijk een been ten honde,
    Zoo smijt gij mij, voor dank,
Wat geld! Te geenen stonde,
    Of ware ik nog zo krank,
En wille ik het! Gaat hene,
       Ten duivel snelt;
Hij breke u hals en schenen:
       't is Judasgeld!

TO...?

As tae a dog a bane
Ye toss me doun some siller,
Thinkin I wad be fain,
Fegs mon, gin I were iller
I'd no tak haud o't. Thanks?
Deil gar ye fash
An' snap hals-bane an' shanks
F'yir Judas cash!

(YL)

Poems originally in English
TO A FRIEND ON THE EVE OF MAY 1858 (in English)

Did we not learn our poetry together?

Faber

Once I see the flowery wreaths of May,
the month of love for Mary and her Child,
the month of love for thee, my pious friend,
the month of love of poetry, more sweet
Than love to both our blended loving hearts!
Once more I see thee, glorious month, ascend
Triumphant in the skies, whom first of all
My eyes did greet when life, bestowed on me
By Him who giveth all, a flowery bud,
Unfolded its fair blossom: when my heart
First beat against the heart that gave it life.
On this fair eve of May, when I was born,
Should I repress the beatings of a heart
That beats for thee, my friend, because it beats
For none but virtuous? ... Should I repel
The sweet remembrance of my childly love
When none I knew but virtuous loving hearts
(No none but a *remembered* priviledge!)?
Should I restrain my love for thee, who art
A child as yet, and much more lovely thus? ...
O, sweet companion of my heart! Forgive
If, on this glorious eve of may, I think
And pray for thee to Her, who took the seat
Of one unhallowed Goddess of the flowers,
Proclaimed by Pagan muse, by Christian Faith
Thrust back into het nothingness! Forgive
If, looking forth into the misty haze
Of future times, I pray for thee to Her!
And if, perchance, thy destined path should lead
Where, priestly friend, I never tread myself,
Remember him, who loved thee like a child

For love of Him, who was a Child Himself!
Remember me, nor do forget the home
Where all who meet shall never have to part!

ARISE YE FLEMINGS! (fragment in English)

Arise, ye Flemings, firm and bold,
be the story never told
that your saxon blood untrue
struggle was too strong for you!

FULL FIFTY YEARS (in English)

Full fifty years your noble heart
in all our bliss and woe took part.
you were our hope, our strength and light,
you led us on and through the fight,
we followed you till Glory came
and laureld your immortal name.

O HOLY PATHMOS (in English)

o Holy Pathmos
Isle of sainted love
Where old Saint John lived
Simple as a dove
Soaring as an eagle
Strong in holy love.

o Holy Pathmos
might it ever be
(that) I should live and die here
only known to Thee
my God and my Saviour
Jesus, might it be?

o Blessed Virgin
Mother of our Lord
Mother whose affliction
Joy to me restored
Pray for me o Virgin
Mother of our Lord.

Pray for me Mother
spotless Virgin pray
that among the scandals
of each passing day
spotless I may love Thee
Holy Mother pray.

Holy apostle
Do remember how
On this isle of Pathmos
thinking of Thee now
I became thy poet
[do remember how].

LADIES AND GENTLEMEN (in English)

Ladies and Gentlemen,
Gentlemen and Ladies,
come and buy, my merchandise
patent cheap well made is;
[come and buy] the peddler boys,
knives and scissors, quickly,
worsted, thread and pretty toys,
pins and needles prickly;
come and buy, the Jubilee,
queen's jubiliee, endeavour
to celebrate right worthily!
Hip hip hourah for ever!

MAY YOUR FRIENDS (in English)

May your friends
both see and hear you
mother dear I
humbly pray
and our Lady blessing rear you
on your festive
Lady day.

KEY TO TRANSLATORS

AB	Adriaan Barnouw
AE	Albert van Eyken
AL	André Lefevere
CS	Carl Stillman
DC	David Colmer
EM	Edwin Morgan
FJ	Francis Jones
GR	Gustave van Roosbroeck
JBi	Jethro Bithell
JBr	James Brockway
JF	Jane Fenoulhet
JH	James Holmes
JI	John Irons
KH	Kenneth Hare
MR	Michael Rigelsford
MS	Maude Swepstone
PC/CD	Paul Claes/Christine D'haen
PK	Peter King
PV	Paul Vincent
TW	Theodoor Weevers
YL	Yann Lovelock

BIBLIOGRAPHY OF ENGLISH TRANSLATIONS OF GEZELLE

(in chronological order of publication)

Kenley, M. (adaptor), *Gezelle Songs*. Antwerp/Brussels: De Vlaamse Muziekhandel/Flandria, 1908.

Bithell, J., *Contemporary Flemish Poetry*. London/New York/Melbourne: Walter Scott Publishing Co. 1917, pp. 48–53: To the Sun, A May Day, The Aspen Tree, Winter Quiet, Palm Sunday.

Dawson, H., in *De Stem uit Belgie*, 16 March 1917, p. 8: The Water Mirror.

Roosbroeck, G.L., *Guido Gezelle – The Mystic Poet of Flanders*. Vinton, Iowa: Kruse, 1919, pp. 35, 39, 40, 41, 42, 43, 45, 48, 49, 51, 53, 54, 55, 56, 61, 65, 68, 72, 73: Once There Fell, The Spade, Out! There They Come All, White as Wool, The Hawthorn, Have Pity, White Lies the Snow, The Nightingale, Evening, O Trees, A Bunch of Cherries, The Sun Arrows, Without Lies, The Cherry Tree, The Child of Death, Joy, The Rustling, The Sun, Ego Flos.

Baker, T., *Two Gezelle Songs of Meditation*. New York: G. Schirmer Inc., 1922.

Opdycke, M.E., *Sacred Songs of Gezelle*. New York: Composers' Music Corporation, 1923.

Cammaerts, E., in *The Treasure House of Belgium*. London: Macmillan, 1924, pp. 21–3, 156–60, 175, 178: O Wild and Unsullied Splendour (fragment), How Still It Is (fragment), How Fair You Are, O Leye (fragment), O Wonderful Willows, Cassel Cows (fragment), May-Tree (fragment), Ego Flos (fragment), Easter, Easter, Loud and Clear (fragment), O Wriggling, Twisting Water-Things, The Nightingale (fragment), O Sweet Flowers of the Summer Gardens (tr. J. Bithell), A Branch of Cherries, Child, Easter Monday.

Clough, S.B., in *A History of the Flemish Movement in Belgium*. New York: Richard R. Smith, 1930, p. 104: My Flanders Speaks a Single Tongue.

Burnet, J., in *The Walburgian,* July 1930: My Heart is Like a Plant, Little, Fragile Reed, The Old Breviary.

Cammaerts, T., in *Anglo-Belgian Notes* (October 1930): A Branch of Cherries, Child.

Backer, F. de, *Contemporary Flemish Literature*. Brussels: PEN Centre. 1934, pp. 16, 18: The Meanest Flower, I Hear the Sounding Horns.

Swepstone, M., *Guido Gezelle (1830–1899). Selection from his Poems, translated into English from the Flemish. With a Short Account of his Life*. Bristol: Burleigh Press, 1937, pp. 5–6, 8, 12–13, 18–54: The Mandel Stream (fragment), Invocation, When the Soul Listens, Oh! The Rustling, Why Cannot We? O Sacred Bell, The Raven, O Golden Head, Skylark Art Thou Called, The Sower, What Is It That Attracts Thee?, Sleep Ye Still?, The Blackbird, My Heart Is Like a Tender Flower, The Cassel Cows, Irrequietum, The Sunflower, Loveliness, Autumn Tints, Two Horses, Snowflakes, The Digger, Tears, This I Fain Would Known, Velut Umbra, Incense, The Weather Witches, The Golden Fleece, Little Mother, Pearls, Marie, The Fir-Tree Branches, Whitsuntide, Sunrise, Ego Flos.

Stillman, C., in *Poet Lore* 47/4 (Winter 1941), 'Six Poets of Belgium', pp. 364, 366: O Rustling of the River Reed, That Evening and that Rose.

Barnouw, A.J., in *Coming After: An Anthology of Poetry from the Low Countries*. New Brunswick, NJ: Rutgers University Press. 1948, pp. 149–63: Our Flemish Speech, O Rustling of the Rushes' Throng, The Last Rite, That Evening and that Rose.

Barnouw, A.J., Hill, F.E., Stillman C., in *Album Dr. Frank Baur*, 2 vols, Antwerp/Brussels/Ghent/Leuven: N.V. StandaardBoekhandel, 1948, I, 159–61: That Evening and that Rose, in F. Closset, 'Drie Amerikaanse vertalingen van Guido Gezelle's "Dien avonde en die rooze"', 158–64.

McCarthy, M.H.P., in F. Closset, 'Nog een vertaling van Guido Gezelle's 'Dien avond en die rooze', *Tijdschrift voor Levende Talen*, 156–9.

Goris, J.-A., in *Belgian Letters*. New York: Belgian Information Centre. 1949, p. 14: That Evening and that Rose (tr. F.E. Hill).

Stillman, C. and F., in *Lyra belgica*. New York: Belgian Government Information Center, 1960, pp. 13–30: That Evening and That Rose, Song, O Rustling of the River Reed, Mother, Why So Slow, Mandel Stream, The Little Writer, Hosannah, Evening, You Prayed Upon the Mount, In the Evening, The Root and the Flower, Ichthus Eis Aiei, I Hear the Sound of Trumpets, Prayer.

Hare, K., in *Nymphs and Rivers*. London: Robert Hale Ltd, 1957, pp. 107–12: The Nightingale, The West Glows Red, I hear You Not Yet, Chantecleere, The Nightingales Are Calling.

Weevers, T., in *Poetry of the Netherlands in its European Context 1170–1930*. London: Athlone Press, 1960, pp. 280–3: Ego Flos (fragment).

Holmes, J.S., in *Delta* (Spring 1961), 30–1: A Bunch of Cherries, Child.

Brockway, J., in *A Sampling of Dutch Literature*. Hilversum: Radio Nederland Wereldomroep, [1962], p. 33: You Prayed On the Mountainside, Alone.

D'haen, C., *Guido Gezelle. Poems*. Deurle: Colibrant, 1971, 108 pp.: Oh Rustling of the Slender Reed, A Bunch of Cherries, Child, The Evening and the Rose, You Prayed Upon a Mount, O Song, How Fare You, The Last, The Tom-Tit Nest, Oh Splendour Wild and Undefiled, The Evening Comes So Still, Oh You Fat ..., My Heart is Like a Blossoming Bush, The Nightingale, I Hear You Not Yet, Easter, Mother, The Old Breviary, The Panes, Mayday, Ichthus eis aiei, Lips of the Rose, Cassel-cows, The Evening-trump, Back, Ego Flos.

D'haen, C., in *Ons Erfdeel* 15/1 (Jan./Feb. 1972), 30: The Evening and the Rose.

Wydouw, U., in *Gezellekroniek* 9 (1974), 143–4: Tears.

Lefevere, A., in *Stand* 18/1 (1977), 51: Beethoven's Septuor.

Denys, K., in *Gezellekroniek* 14 (1980), 107: *When the Soul is List'ning (previously published in Gazette van Detroit)*

Lefevere, A., in *Dutch Crossing* 12 (December 1980), 30–3: Where Sits that Limpid Singer.

Eyken, A. van, in *Dutch Crossing* 35 (August 1988), 'Guido Gezelle – Poet, Priest, Patriot', 60–93: Hark! 't the Wind, Pagan Song, Sighing Reed, Wasted Effort, How Still!, Poplar Trees, Church Window, Evening, How Lightly is the Burning Brand, That Evening, O Friends, be Kind!, Yearning.

Claes, P. and D'haen, C., *The Evening and the Rose: 30 Poems translated from the Flemish.* Antwerp: Guido Gezellegenootschap, 1989, 115 pp.: O Trembling of the Tender Reed, In the White Moon Winking, A Bunch of Cherries, Child, The Evening and the Rose, There Fell a Leaflet, The Tom-Tit Nest, Sharp Needles Pierce the Sky, The Evening Comes So Still, So Still, O Splendour Wild and Undefiled, O You Fat ..., My Heart is Like a Flowerage, Where Sits that Limpid Singer, I Hear You Not Yet, Mother, O Leak of Light, I Never Eat but What I Eat, The Panes, Sleeping Buds, May-Day, Ichtys eis Aiei, Cassel-Cows, May-Song, Rosy-Mouth, Winter Midges, Tears, Back, In Speculo, Jam Sol Recedit, Swifts, Ego Flos.

Claes, P. and D'haen, C., in *The Low Countries* 1 (1993–4), 142: The Evening and the Rose.

Nuis, H.J. van, in *Guido Gezelle, Flemish Poet-Priest.* New York/Westport, Conn./London: Greenwood Press, 1986, pp. 23, 24, 26, 28, 29, 33, 42, 46, 48, 50, 51, 55, 56: Principium, Message of the Birds, Water Beetle, In the Silence of the Night, To the Skylark, Graveyard Flowers, Visiting the Holy of Holies, *Rammentati,* I Miss You, Jesu (all fragments).

*

LISTS OF PUBLISHED TRANSLATIONS

ARENTS, P., *De Vlaamse schrijvers in het Engels vertaald, 1481–1949*. Gent: Koninklijke Vlaamse Akademie, 1950.

HERMANOWSKI, G. and H. TOMME, *Zuidnederlandse literatuur in vertaling, 1900–1960*. Hasselt: Heideland, 1961.

BIBLIOGRAPHY OF SECONDARY LITERATURE ON GEZELLE IN ENGLISH

(in chronological order of publication)

BITHELL, J., *Contemporary Belgian Literature*. London: T. Fisher Unwin, 1915, pp. 16, 23, 25, 26, 42, 43, 315.
ROOSBROECK, G.L. van, *Guido Gezelle. The Mystic Poet of Flanders*. Vinton, Iowa: Kruse, 1919.
CAMMAERTS, E., in *The Treasure House of Belgium*. London: MacMillan & Co., 1924, pp. 6, 7, 21–3, 52, 98, 153, 155–60, 162, 164, 175, 178.
BURNET, J., 'Guido Gezelle. An Appreciation', *The Walburgian*, July 1930, 108–12.
BURNET, J., 'The Flower Poet of Flanders', *The Walburgian*, January 1931, 15–16.
FARQUHARSON SHARP, R., *A Short Biographical Dictionary of Foreign Literature*, London/New York: J.M. Dent & Sons Ltd/E.P. Dutton & Co.Inc. 1933, p. 99.
SMITH, H. (ed.), *Columbia Dictionary of Modern European Literature*. New York: Columbia University Press, 1947, pp. 320–1.
STEINBERG, S.H. (ed.), *Cassell's Enyclopaedia of Literature*, 2 vols. London: Cassell, 1953, I, 936–7.
WEEVERS, T., *Poetry of the Netherlands in its European Context 11701930*. London: Athlone Press, 1960, pp.vi, xii, 5, 147, 156–61, 176, 278–82
KUNITZ, S.J. and V. COLBY, *European Authors 1000–1900*, New York: The H.W. Wilson Co. 1967, pp. 325–6.
THORLBY, A. (ed.), *The Penguin Companion to Literature*, 4 vols. Harmondsworth: Penguin Books, 1969, II, 309.
SEYMOUR-SMITH, M., *Guide to Modern World Literature*. London: Wolf Publishing Ltd, 1973, pp. 370–1.
MEIJER, R.P., *Literature of the Low Countries*. Cheltenham: Stanley Thornes, 1978, pp. 233–6, 247, 282, 315, 371.
KING, P.K., *Gezelle and Multatuli: A Question of Social History*. Hull: University of Hull (Inaugural Lecture), 1978.

NUIS, H.J. van, *Guido Gezelle, Flemish Poet-Priest*. New York/Greenwood, Conn./London: Greenwood Press, 1986.

GORING, R., (ed.) *Larousse Dictionary of Writers*. Edinburgh/New York: Larousse, 1994, p. 362.

HENDERSON, L. (ed.) *Reference Guide to World Literature*, 2 vols, New York/London, etc., 1995, I, 465–6.

Encyclopedia Britannica (latest book and CD-ROM edition), reference in 'Flemish Literature'.

Microsoft Encarta 99 (CD-ROM), reference in 'Flemish Literature'.

Lightning Source UK Ltd.
Milton Keynes UK
UKHW012145050320
359859UK00001B/73